The Super Prestige Series

OLDHAM

Colin Reeve

ISBN 978 1905 304 462

Acknowledgements

When I was asked to write a book on Oldham Transport I jumped at the chance as I have been associated with the area in one way or another for most of my life. As a schoolboy I travelled on service 12 between Middleton and Boundary Park to watch Oldham Athletic and by North Western to Diggle where we lived for a short time. Then later as a scheduler at Manchester Corporation I worked with my opposite numbers at Oldham on joint services and at weekends drove red buses deep into Oldham territory to exotic destinations such as Waterhead, Greenfield and Newhey.

In writing this book I have had a great deal of help from many people. Thanks go especially to David Bielby and Keith Hampton for sharing their extensive knowledge of North Western operations in Oldham and Saddleworth and correcting some of my misconceptions and to John Holmes for his extensive personal knowledge of Oldham's operations in the post-war years. John Holmes, Geoff Lumb, Tony Moyes and John Senior supplied innumerable photographs from their collections including many from the late Geoff Hyde, and George Turnbull allowed me the run of the Greater Manchester Transport Museum archives, so much so that I had far more pictures than I could use. For this I apologise. Thanks also to the staff at the Oldham Local Studies Library and Archive who helped me to delve into the minutes of the Tramways and Passenger Transport Committees and sub-Committees.

Colin Reeve
Rochdale February 2012

Photo credits

AM Tony Moyes
CR Colin Reeve
DBC David Bielby Collection
JAS John Senior
JJH John Holmes
MMT Greater Manchester Museum of Transport
OLS Oldham Local Studies and Archive
RLS Rochdale Library Services
STA Senior Transport Archive

CONTENTS

Introduction

OLDHAM

The town of Oldham stands on a windy hilltop on the edge of the Pennines approximately seven miles north-east of Manchester city centre and some 500 feet above it. The name is said to derive from the Norse 'Ald Holm', meaning 'High Hill', which is certainly appropriate. Oldham has little early history and before the Industrial Revolution was not much more than a handful of small settlements scattered along the former Roman road, now the A62 from Manchester to York, through what was then known as Oldham Below to distinguish it from the upper town known as Oldham Above.

Probably the town's most famous son was Hugh Oldham, born about 1452, who became Bishop of Exeter and in 1515 founded Manchester Grammar School. The Oldham family arms, depicting three owls, was adopted both by the school and later by the new Borough of Oldham, an interesting play on words as the town was long known in the Lancashire dialect as Owldham.

Oldham rose to prominence during the late eighteenth century as a centre of textile manufacturing and associated engineering industries, rapidly becoming one of the most important centres of the cotton industry in England. At its zenith Oldham was said to be the most productive cotton spinning mill town in the world, spinning more cotton than the whole of France and Germany put together, although with the decline in heavy industry it has moved towards the service sector and is now largely residential, lying as it does within easy commuting distance of Manchester.

Oldham became a Parliamentary Borough in 1832, a Municipal Borough in 1849 and a County Borough 40 years later. In 1974 it became a Metropolitan Borough within the then Metropolitan County of Greater Manchester, absorbing the ring of small towns around it that had always looked to Oldham for their services, but also including the district of Saddleworth in the West Riding of Yorkshire whose inhabitants were so loyal to the white rose that rather than shop in nearby Oldham they would often take the North Western or the Hanson bus across Standedge to Huddersfield. Oldham is now a

This view of the Market Place during the First World War shows tram 103, which has now received a top cover, just arriving from Manchester on its way to Waterhead. The policeman on the left and the inspector on the right are both watching the woman cross the track. The line to the left goes down George Street to the Star Inn. ***(STA)***

Unitary Authority with a population of some 217,000 at the last census.

Before the Industrial Revolution highways were little more than cart tracks, often all but impassable in bad weather, but with booming industry and a growing population improved transport links were becoming ever more important and this need led to the creation of turnpikes, roads which were improved and kept repaired out of tolls collected at gates or Turn Pikes along the route. From the middle of the 18th century Oldham became the hub of a network of turnpike roads radiating from the town to Manchester, Middleton, Rochdale and Ashton and across the Pennines into Yorkshire to Halifax and Huddersfield.

While Oldham's hilltop site made it unsuitable for canals, there were several examples in the surrounding area. First came the Hollinwood Branch Canal, a 4½-mile spur from the Ashton Canal to Hollinwood, then a small village south of the town on the way to Manchester. It opened in 1795, its main purpose being to carry coal from the many small mines to the south of Oldham, although passengers were also conveyed. The Rochdale Canal from Manchester to Yorkshire opened in 1804 and skirted the town through Chadderton a couple of miles to the west. The Huddersfield Narrow Canal, on which work had started in 1794, finally opened in 1811, running up the valley of the River Tame from Ashton-under-Lyne through Mossley, Uppermill and the Standedge Tunnel.

The Manchester and Leeds Railway opened a branch from its main line at Middleton Junction to Werneth in 1842, the 1 in 27 gradient making this the steepest conventional railway line in the country. Five years later it was extended to Mumps. The London and North Western Railway opened a branch from its Manchester to Huddersfield line at Greenfield through Lees to Oldham in 1856 and the Oldham, Ashton-under-Lyne and Guide Bridge Railway, jointly owned by the London and North Western and the Great Central, arrived in the town in 1861. Finally, in 1880 the Lancashire and Yorkshire Railway, the successor to the Manchester and Leeds, completed the local network when it opened a new direct link from Oldham to Manchester via Hollinwood. There were now five railway stations in the town at Werneth, Central, Clegg Street, Mumps and Glodwick Road.

The Market Place in the immediate pre-war period showing a tram on its way to Waterhead and a Roe-bodied Leyland Titan double-decker on service 3. ***(STA)***

2 – *HORSES AND STEAM*

The improvements in the roads generated by the turnpikes resulted in the development of coach services and sometime after 1820 a coach ran regularly between Oldham and Ashton, although at fares which the average working man could not afford. The first horse bus service in Oldham started running in 1861 between the town and Rochdale although it was short-lived. It was followed in June 1863 by a service between Manchester and Chapel Road just north of Hollinwood and some two miles south of the town centre. This ran for a number of years before being superceded by the trams of the Manchester Carriage Company. In the next few years two other services began, from Oldham to Lees and to Shaw but little is known about them.

By the Tramways Act of 1870, which authorised the promotion of street tramways, local authorities were enabled to construct and own tramways but were not allowed to operate them and were obliged to lease them to private companies. The first lines in Oldham were authorised by the Oldham Borough Tramways Order of 1878 and consisted of a standard 4ft 8½in gauge horse-drawn tramway from Hollinwood to Asa Lees Iron Works via Manchester Road and Huddersfield Road with trams travelling through Oldham town centre either by the Market Place or along Union Street.

The route was soon extended to Waterhead and a car shed and stables were built for the operation at Stable Street in Hollinwood. The track was completed by September 1880 and was leased for a period of 21 years to the Manchester Carriage and Tramways Company which had just been formed by the amalgamation of the two major operators in the Manchester area, the Manchester Carriage Company and the Manchester Suburban Tramways Company, then running a network of horse tram services extending over a large area of the Manchester conurbation. The Hollinwood depot, one of five in the Company's Oldham and Openshaw Division, housed 28 cars and had 267 stalls for the horses, the feed being supplied from a granary at the main depot at Newton Heath. The cars were painted in a bright red and white livery which was adopted by Manchester Corporation when it took over much of the Company's operation in 1901.

A service of horse trams commenced on 1st November 1880, later connecting at Hollinwood with the Company's trams from there to Manchester when they started running on 28th March 1881. The cars were of the Eades Patent Reversible type, named after its inventor John Eades, the Works Manager of the Manchester Company, the single-ended body being mounted on a turntable carried on the truck. This could be turned round at the end of the journey with the horses still in harness without the need for expensive reversing facilities and the elimination of the second staircase on double-deckers saved weight and allowed more passengers to be carried. Both single-deck and double-deck versions operated on the route. The service ran until 31st October 1901 when the lease expired.

The Manchester, Bury, Rochdale and Oldham Steam Tramways Company (MBRO) was formed in 1881 as part of a much larger scheme for a network of steam tramways across south east Lancashire. The lines in Oldham were authorised by the Oldham Borough Tramways (Extension) Order of 1882, which empowered the Council to construct and maintain, but not operate, a line 2¼ miles in length from the Royton boundary in the north along Oldham Road and Ashton Road to the boundary of the then Limehurst Rural District at Fir Tree Avenue, Hathershaw in the south. In addition there was to be a branch line one mile in length from Rochdale Road along Featherstall Road to Platt's Ironworks at Werneth on the Manchester route to serve heavy peak hour workmen's traffic in the area. Additional lines from Rochdale to Oldham via Milnrow, Newhey and Shaw and from Oldham to Lees were also considered but powers were never sought.

The tracks were to be built to the standard 4ft 8½in gauge and it was originally intended to operate the service through from Rochdale, but due to narrow streets in the area the Board of Trade decreed that, to maintain statutory clearances, the lines in Rochdale should be constructed to the narrower 3ft 6in gauge. Oldham Council, however, insisted that the tracks within the Borough be to standard gauge which was the same as that of the horse trams, and the promoters, with their sights set on eventual through running to Manchester, did not disagree. This resulted in a break in the service at the old toll bar at Dogford Lane (later renamed Dogford Road), Royton and a depot

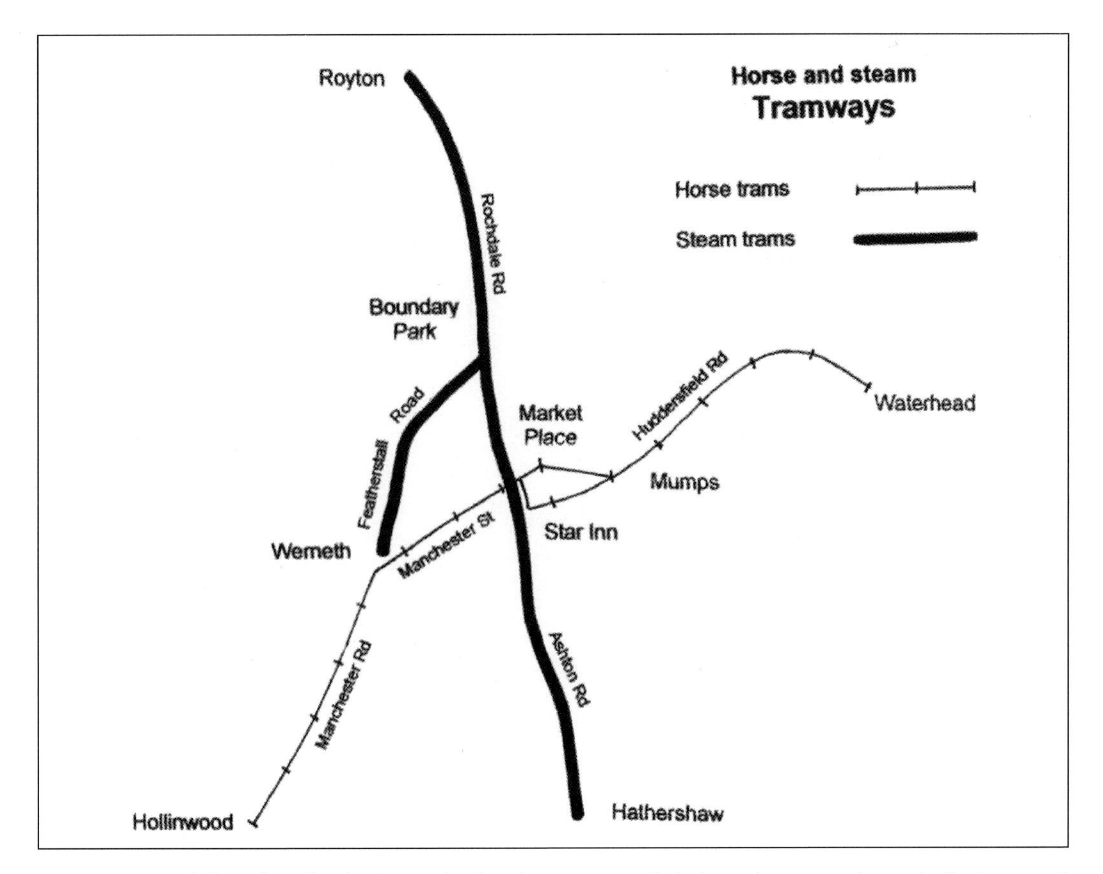

was constructed there housing both standard and narrow gauge rolling stock side by side.

A service of steam trams commenced on 1st August 1885 from Dogford Lane through the town centre to Hathershaw, but the line along Featherstall Road to Werneth did not open until 4th July 1889. Both engines and passenger cars were smartly painted in brown with black and white lining, although this deteriorated rapidly with the effect of smoke, neglect and the Lancashire weather. The MBRO eventually became the second largest steam tramway in Britain, running 91 locomotives and 81 trailers on 30 miles of route. The Company was owned by Henry Osborne O'Hagan, a flamboyant London entrepreneur, and was run as a subsidiary of his City of London Contract Corporation, which took all the profits as management fees, thereby making O'Hagan rich but leaving nothing for maintenance or replacement of assets, nor anything for the local shareholders.

This financial chicanery resulted in the rapid deterioration of the track and rolling stock and in 1888 the Manchester, Bury, Rochdale and Oldham Steam Tramways Company went bankrupt, the network being taken over by a similarly named company omitting Manchester from its title. Things got no better and in July 1898 Oldham decided to promote a Bill in Parliament to obtain powers to operate its own services when the lease ran out, again on 30th October 1901. However, this was not possible immediately and agreement was reached whereby the Company continued running for a time, paying rent to the Corporation on a weekly basis.

The last steam trams ran on 30th May 1904, their passing regretted by few. They were noisy and dirty, emitting sparks and smoke and showering their surroundings with ashes and soot. As the neglected track led to more and more noise and vibration most people were glad to see them go. The Royton depot was then used for storing withdrawn cars awaiting disposal. Oldham Corporation later used the premises for garaging buses until the opening of the new depot on Henshaw Street in 1926. The site was subsequently used for light industrial units, part of the old car shed still existing in 2011 although much modified in the intervening years.

Single-deck Eades car number O.78 of the Manchester Carriage and Tramways Company, the O prefix identifying it as belonging to the Company's Oldham and Openshaw Division. ***(STA)***

In this busy scene at Rhodes Bank a double-deck Eades car working from Waterhead to the Market Place, climbs the hill from Mumps and takes the right fork up Yorkshire Street. The line to the right of the picture runs along Union Street. A similar car, L.53, is preserved in full working order at the Heaton Park Tramway. ***(STA)***

Number 88, one of a pair of horizontal-boilered Beyer Peacock locomotives, pulls a Falcon trailer car through Royton town centre on its way to Hathershaw. ***(STA)***

Another Beyer Peacock locomotive stands on Featherstall Road at the Werneth terminus of the route from Royton. ***(STA)***

Locomotive number 54, a horizontal-boilered Manning Wardle engine dating from 1885, stands at the Hathershaw terminus on the last day of service, 30th May 1904. ***(STA)***

The Royton depot closed its doors to steam in January 1905. More than a century later some of the buildings still remain; although over the years there have been many alterations and additions to adapt them for their present use as a home for a number of small businesses. The picture shows the former narrow gauge car shed on Schofield Street, the lower extension on the left, over what was originally open sidings, being a later addition. Trams on the Oldham route would have travelled further up the street before turning into the standard gauge depot. ***(CR)***

3 – *ELECTRIC TRAMS*

The 1899 Act

While all this was going on, things were happening in the neighbouring town of Middleton which were to help shape the future of public transport in Oldham. In October 1897 the British Electric Traction Company, which was currently in the process of promoting electric tramways throughout the country, applied for powers under the 1896 Light Railways Act to construct a network of lines centred on Middleton, one of which would extend through Chadderton to Oldham. The application was heard by the Light Railways Commissioners at an Enquiry held in Middleton on 5th February 1898 and despite objections from Oldham on the grounds that they were themselves considering applying to construct and operate tramways within the Borough, the application was granted.

Oldham appealed to the Board of Trade who accepted their arguments and ruled that the company could not construct lines in Oldham without Oldham's consent for two years after the commencement of the order and if during that time Oldham built the lines themselves the powers would lapse. The Order commenced on 15th December 1898 which gave Oldham until 15th December 1900 to complete the work.

Spurred on by these events, Oldham decided to promote their own Bill to take over and electrify the horse and steam tramways when their leases expired and to construct and operate their own tramways in the Borough. The Bill passed quickly through the Parliamentary procedures and duly became the Oldham Corporation Act of 1899, which authorised the following new lines:

- Along Chadderton Road to the Chadderton boundary at Westhulme Avenue,
- Along Middleton Road to the Chadderton boundary at Neville Street,
- Along Union Street West,
- Along Hollins Road and Copster Hill Road between Manchester Road and Ashton Road,
- Along Hollins Road South between Hollins Road and Ashton Road,
- Along Park Road, Glodwick Road and Cross Street between Ashton Road and Huddersfield Road,
- Along Lees Road to the Lees boundary at Brook Side,
- Along Ripponden Road to Moorside,
- Along Shaw Road to the Royton boundary at Higginshaw Road,
- Along Egerton Street to Shaw Road and
- A number of streets and connections in the town centre.

The line along Hollins Road South was never built and the Egerton Street route was closed quite early but, together with the former horse and steam tram routes, the network within the Borough was now established in the form it would take for the life of the tramways.

Now the Act was passed things began to move quickly. Members of the newly constituted Surveyor's and Tramways Committee travelled to Liverpool in September 1899 to inspect that city's tramways and as a result tenders were invited for track and equipment. The following January they also visited Manchester to look at the new tramcars that had just been delivered there and the Borough Surveyor was instructed to prepare designs for a suitable car for operation in Oldham.

With the time limit imposed by the Board of Trade, the first priority was the Middleton Road route and on 6th February 1900 construction commenced on a single track line with four passing loops. The overhead wire was carried on ornate brackets attached to side poles with the electrical equipment supplied by WT Glover and Co. of Trafford Park. The ornate scrollwork was copied on successive construction but was later removed when it was found to retain rainwater leading to corrosion of the poles. A small depot was built at the Chadderton end of the line to house the cars working the route.

Although the Borough Surveyor had recommended the purchase of four single-truck open-top double-deck cars the Committee, after much deliberation, decided instead to obtain one each to four different specifications, the order going to the Electric Railway and Tramway Carriage Works Ltd of Preston. Numbers 1 and 2 were respectively a single-decker and a double-decker built on a single Brill 21E truck, number 3 was a double-decker on Brill 22E bogies and number 4 a single-decker on Brill 27G bogies. All had electrical equipment by Dick Kerr.

The cars, which were painted dark blue, were delivered early in November by which time the track and the depot were complete and ready for use. The Board of Trade inspection was carried out on 22nd November 1900 by Lt. Col. PG von Donop who, mindful of the ruling 1 in 25 gradient on the line, ordered that track brakes should be fitted to the cars before he would issue the necessary certificate. However, it was some time before the job was done, and then only after the service was already running and the Board of Trade had threatened to close down the operation unless Oldham complied. The line was officially opened on 15th December 1900, the deadline imposed at the Appeal Hearing two years earlier.

The trams were fitted with destination indicators at each end with another on either side of the body below the lower saloon windows.

The Next Steps

The Middleton Electric Traction Company's line through Chadderton did not open until 27th March 1902, after which connections became available with the Oldham trams, although to judge by the number of complaints in the local press this did not always happen.

From the beginning the planning and construction of the tramway had been the responsibility of the Borough Surveyor, but now the system was operating a new post of Tramway Superintendent was created and Mr Richard Henry Wilkinson was appointed to the position at a salary of £200 per year. Mr Wilkinson had trained as a marine engineer and came from Liverpool where he was currently Assistant to the General Manager of Liverpool Corporation Tramways. In February 1902 he was promoted to General Manager, his salary being increased to £300.

Soon after the construction of the Middleton Road line had got under way, work was started on the next three routes. These were, Park Road/ Glodwick Road, Lees Road, and Hollins Road/ Copster Hill Road. Twelve new cars, generally similar to Number 4, were ordered, again from the Electric Railway and Tramway Carriage Works. These were numbered 5 to 16 and were painted in a rich red-brown livery, sometimes referred to as maroon or crimson lake that was to become standard from then on.

The first two routes were inspected by Major E Druitt on 24th May 1901. The hilly nature of the town is evident in their ruling gradients, 1 in 13.8 on Glodwick Road and 1 in 13.6 on Lees Road which together with sharp bends resulted in his imposing severe speed restrictions as low as 4 mph in some places and again insisting on the fitting of track brakes. The lines were officially opened by Alderman Eckersley, the Chairman of the Tramways Committee on 15th June 1901. Major Druitt visited Oldham again on 18th July to inspect the Hollins Road and Copster Hill Road section, noting a gradient of 1 in 13.4 and again imposing severe speed limits and the fitting of track brakes. The service commenced on 29th August, for the time being trams operating from temporary depots on Glodwick Road and Copster Hill Road. The routes were colour coded with coloured lights and discs being displayed at each end of the car.

Conversions

While these latest routes were still under construction it had been decided that the next phase would be the electrification and integration of the horse and steam tram routes after their leases ran out on 31st October 1901. Oldham was now running 16 trams from three temporary depots on isolated sections of route separated by the company tracks and this state of affairs could not continue indefinitely. More trams were ordered from the same builder, comprising ten single-deckers numbered 17-26 and 54 double-deckers numbered 27-80, all on Brill 21E trucks with Dick Kerr electrical equipment. These cars were all delivered during 1902 and 1903. A permanent depot to house 80 cars, together with office accommodation, was built at Wallshaw Street near Mumps Bridge.

The last day of horse tram operation was 31st October 1901 and work started the following day on converting the route from Waterhead through to Hollinwood for the electric cars, no less than 900 men being employed on the project. The work took over six months to complete, the whole of the route being left without any form of transport for all that time, while much of the town centre was severely disrupted for lengthy periods. The public were not amused and vented their feelings in the correspondence pages of the *Oldham Chronicle*.

By contrast the conversion of the former steam

tramway was carried out in stages, the first section being along Ashton Road from the Star Inn to Copster Hill Road which was completed on 12th March 1902 and enabled the isolated lengths of line along Hollins Road and Copster Hill Road and along Park Road and Glodwick Road to be connected to Ashton Road and through services to be run from the Star Inn.

Public services between Hollinwood and Waterhead recommenced on 17th May 1902 with the formal opening two days later. Eight decorated cars carried members of the Council and invited guests from the Town Hall to Hollinwood via Manchester Road, returning via Hollins Road, Copster Hill Road, Ashton Road, Union Street and Huddersfield Road to Waterhead. The convoy then returned to the new Wallshaw Street depot where the Mayor, Alderman Eckersley, unveiled a marble tablet commemorating the event. The Carriage Company continued to run horse trams between Hollinwood and Manchester until 31st March 1903, the electric cars of Manchester Corporation taking over the following day, but it would be some time before through running between Waterhead and Manchester was reinstated.

On 22nd May the Ashton Road line was extended at both ends, from the Star Inn to Middleton Road and from Copster Hill Road to the Borough boundary at Hathershaw. Then on 9th June through running commenced between Lees Road and Hollinwood via Werneth.

The network grows

At their meeting on 6th May 1902, the Tramways Committee agreed a programme for completing the conversion of the steam tram routes and constructing the remaining lines authorised in the 1899 Act, these being along Shaw Road to the Borough boundary at Higginshaw together with the branch along Egerton Street, and along Ripponden Road as far as Moorside.

Major Druitt inspected the tracks on 29th August 1902 and there would appear to have been some unwanted problems as the *Oldham Chronicle* reported that the car carrying the inspector left the rails near the Egerton Arms and also that the trolley left the wire on several occasions. Nonetheless, with a few speed restrictions on tight corners the route was passed and the Shaw Road service commenced the following day. However, due to a temporary shortage of trams, the ill-fated service along Egerton Street was not introduced until 4th September and following problems with frontagers which interrupted the operation it was soon withdrawn.

At the same time the reconstructed former steam tramway was extended along Rochdale Road to the Royton boundary at Sheepfoot Lane and the opportunity was taken to change the route pattern. The Hathershaw to Chadderton Road service was split in the town centre and new cross town services were introduced between Middleton Road and Higginshaw via Park Road and between Hathershaw and Royton. The Ripponden Road line opened to Moorside on 18th October and the former steam line along Featherstall Road on 19th November. On 11th December 1902 the line along Union Street was completed and the Glodwick service became a circular.

The tramway network within the Borough was now basically complete, the services and colour codes being as follows:

Route	Colour
• Waterhead-Werneth-Hollinwood	Red
• Lees Road-Werneth-Hollinwood	White
• Star Inn-Middleton Rd	Red
• Glodwick Circular	Violet
• Moorside-Hollins Rd-Hollinwood	Green
• Hathershaw-Boundary Park	Orange
• Werneth-Boundary Park	Red/Green
• Chadderton Road-Higginshaw	Yellow
• Union St West-Waterhead	Red/Green
• Market Place-Egerton St-Higginshaw	White

Some of the longer routes were worked initially in two overlapping sections.

One of the biggest complaints about double-deck trams was the open top deck, especially in a town like Oldham where wind and rain combined to make for an unpleasant ride. So the Council discussed the question of enclosing the upper deck and at the end of 1902 the Tramways Committee paid another visit to Liverpool, this time to look at one of that undertaking's top-covered cars. They were obviously impressed with what they saw as on their return they instructed the General Manager to fit one of the single-deck bogie cars with a covered upper deck and to arrange for one of the new cars on order to be fitted with a Bellamy-type top-cover, named after the Liverpool General Manager who had designed it.

Two of the prototype electric cars are pictured here. Number 2 *(above)* was a double-decker on a Brill 21E truck and number 4 *(below)* was a single-decker on Brill 27G bogies. Both were supplied by the Electric Railway and Tramway Carriage Company of Preston which built the bodies and which would eventually become part of the English Electric Company. Number 2 evolved into Oldham's standard design of double-decker, which by stages acquired first top covers with open balcony ends, then vestibuled platforms and eventually became fully enclosed. Many of the earlier cars were converted to later specifications. Number 2 was fitted with a top cover in 1920 and withdrawn in this form in 1935. Number 4 was the forerunner of a further 22 similar cars, but bogie single-deckers were not popular in Oldham and this car was withdrawn as early as 1916 and sold to Rotherham Corporation. ***(both STA)***

The next twelve single-deckers, numbers 5 to 16, were delivered in 1902. They are seen above forming a train leaving the ERTCC factory in Preston behind a Lancashire and Yorkshire Railway 0-6-0 on the way to Mumps where they would be towed across the road to the newly built depot at Wallshaw Street.

Trams had been running on various small sections of route for up to 18 months and the main line between Waterhead and Hollinwood had opened on 17th May 1902 after its conversion from horse-tram operation. However, the formal opening of the Oldham electric tramway system took place two days later on Whit Monday when eight of the new double-deck cars, suitably decorated for the occasion, lined up outside Oldham Town Hall before taking civic dignitaries and other guests on a tour of the system. The picture has been touched up with 'MUMPS' written in by hand on the destination box of the leading car. ***(both STA)***

The new double-decker, number 76, was delivered in August 1903. With 50 seats and open platforms and stairs it was an immediate success. The single-deck car, number 13, went back into service a month later as a 72-seat double-decker and due to its huge size and height it rapidly became known locally as 'Big Ben'.

Also in 1903 the Corporation took delivery of two service cars, a snow plough and a water tank car for cleaning dirt out of the track grooves. Neither was numbered but the water car later became 38 after the original car bearing that number was withdrawn.

Beyond the boundaries

As far back as 1901 there had been a scheme for tramways in Springhead and Saddleworth connecting with the proposed Oldham lines at their boundary with Lees, a small Urban District squeezed between Oldham and the Yorkshire boundary at County End. Lees wanted the tramway in their area and were prepared to build the line but preferred it to be run by Oldham rather than a private company. This was agreed in principle in October 1902 and Lees obtained authority under the Lees Urban District Council Tramways Order 1902 for the building of the line as well as a branch northwards towards Waterhead which was never built. Construction began on 15th June 1903 and on 1st August that year the Lees Road route was extended from its existing terminus at Brook Side to County End, a distance of less than half a mile, the first time that Oldham's trams had operated outside the Borough. The track was owned by Lees and leased to Oldham for a period of 21 years.

But while Oldham's electric trams were carrying large numbers of passengers and on that account were considered a great success, all was not well on the financial side. At the May 1903 Council meeting it was reported that the new tramways had lost some £10,000 in the previous financial year, something like £650,000 at today's prices! A council audit pinpointed serious overspending on track construction and a lack of cost control within the Borough Surveyor's Department. The Borough Surveyor was dismissed and the department reorganised, and the Council applied to the Board of Trade for borrowing powers to cover the additional costs. In the meantime economy measures were quickly drawn up and on 18th May service cuts were introduced which reduced the turnout by 14 cars from 56 to 42.

The following year the Council decided on more cost-cutting measures including reducing the number of workmen's services and axing the troublesome Egerton Street line altogether, the revisions coming into operation on 14th April 1904.

In September 1904 the General Manager, Mr Wilkinson, resigned to take up a similar position at Huddersfield. His replacement was Mr Lewis Slattery. Born in 1868 he had begun his transport career in 1884 as a clerk with the Bury, Rochdale and Oldham Steam Tramways Company and had then occupied supervisory posts at Hartlepool and Blackburn before becoming General Manager of the Blackpool, St Anne's and Lytham Company in 1896. He took over his duties at Oldham on 11th September 1904.

Two other neighbouring Urban Districts, Royton and Crompton were also interested in electric tramways, Royton of course already having experience of steam tramway operation. The two districts worked closely together and both obtained powers to construct lines in 1901, Royton for the length of Shaw Side between Oldham's terminus at Higginshaw and their boundary with Crompton and along Shaw Road between the steam tramway on Oldham Road and the Crompton boundary at Cowlishaw, and Crompton for the lines from these two points through Shaw town centre to the Wren's Nest. Oldham agreed to lease and operate the lines although there was a problem with Royton who wanted the price of the lease to reflect their purchase of the steam tramway tracks. Agreement could not be reached on the value and the matter eventually went to arbitration.

Although the powers had been obtained construction was delayed by the dispute and it was over two years before work actually commenced, initially on the former steam tracks. The last steam tram ran on Trinity Monday 30th May 1904 and work began to convert the line beyond Boundary Park to electric operation, a through service between Hathershaw and Summit starting on 1st November 1904.

Meanwhile work was progressing on the extension of the Higginshaw route to Shaw, the

Tram number 13 was one of the first production batch of single-deck bogie cars delivered in 1901. The following year it was rebuilt as a double-decker in the Corporation's workshops. It is seen in this form outside Platt's Iron Works on Featherstall Road about 1921 while working on the former steam tram route from Shaw to Hollinwood. The picture gives some idea of the number of workers employed in heavy industry in the area at the time. ***(STA)***

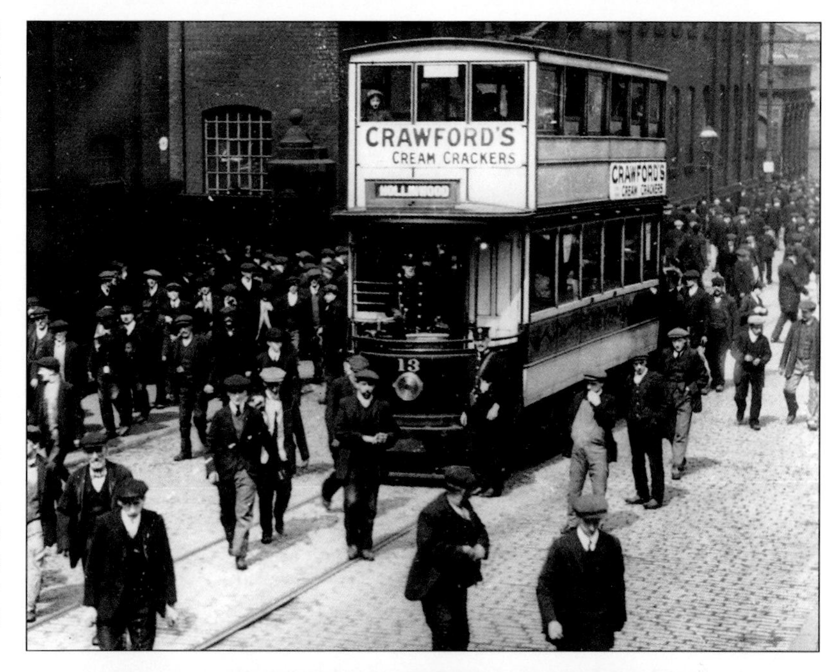

In 1906 the tram services of Oldham and Rochdale Corporations were linked at Thornham Summit to provide a through service between the two towns. This resulted in Rochdale trams running through to Hathershaw and Oldham's cars appearing in the semi-rural setting of Norden where car number 48 is pictured at the terminus outside the Bridge Inn. ***(STA)***

Board of Trade inspection taking place on 9th November 1904 and a through service from Chadderton to Shaw (Wren's Nest) commencing eight days later. Work started on Shaw Road on 9th February 1905, the inspection taking place on the afternoon of 13th April, enabling the Werneth to Boundary Park service to be extended to Shaw town centre later that day.

Through running

Until their demise horse and steam trams had provided through services between Waterhead and Manchester, and between parts of Royton and Rochdale. Their subsequent conversion to electric traction had broken these links and now that the rebuilding was completed pressure built up for their restoration.

The first to be considered, initially for a trial period of twelve months, was the Rochdale route and on 1st May 1906 the services of Oldham and Rochdale Corporations were linked at Thornham Summit to provide through journeys between Hathershaw, Oldham, Rochdale and on to Norden, then a small Urban District on the far side of Rochdale. Oldham was unable to operate its top-covered cars on the service due to the low bridge carrying the Lancashire and Yorkshire Railway line from Manchester to Leeds across Oldham Road at the east end of Rochdale station so that either single-deck or open-top cars had to be used.

The question of restoring the through service to Manchester had first been raised back in 1903 at the time that Manchester had started running its electric trams to Hollinwood. Agreement had been reached in principle between the two Corporations, but now the Failsworth Urban District objected. Failsworth, which lay between Oldham and Manchester, owned the tracks and leased them to Manchester, but contended that the agreement had not included linking the tracks to those of Oldham and operating through services. The dispute appeared to be more of an attempt to put pressure on to Manchester to improve the terms of the lease than a serious objection and a compromise was eventually reached. However, the service did not start for some time owing to the Board of Trade's refusal to allow Manchester cars to operate in Oldham until they too were fitted with track brakes.

Through running commenced on 21st July 1907 when convoys of decorated trams left both Oldham and Manchester and met at Hollinwood where they stood side by side on adjacent tracks while the Lord Mayor of Manchester cut a ribbon stretched across the road and the Oldham Police Band played 'See the Conquering Hero comes.'

The start of the new service prompted requests from Lees and Shaw for similar through facilities, but both were turned down and it would be a number of years before either got its service to Manchester and then it would be by express bus.

The 1909 Act

In October 1907 Oldham Council received a petition from local residents for the Moorside service to be extended to Grains Bar, the furthest north point in Oldham as well as, at 1,115 ft, its highest. While the Council agreed that the extension was desirable, the economics of building and running a tramway to serve what was little more than a handful of cottages were not attractive, so they decided to look instead at using a motor bus to provide a feeder service. The Chairman and General Manager subsequently visited the London Motor Exhibition to look at which buses were available and reported back that they were noisy, smelly and unreliable and cost more than a comparable tramcar both to buy and to run. Consequently, it was agreed to extend the tram tracks, but due to the somewhat precarious financial position this would not happen for a number of years.

The following year Oldham placed a Bill before Parliament to enable them to operate motor omnibuses within the Borough and which, in addition to short sections of track in the town centre, would authorise two new sections of tramway. These were the extension of the Ripponden Road line from Moorside to Grains Bar mentioned above, and a branch from the Hollinwood route at Werneth along Oxford Street to the Chadderton boundary at Block Lane. Chadderton intended to promote its own Bill to extend the route on their side of the boundary, but this did not materialise and the line was never built, eventually becoming a bus route. The Bill went on to the Statute Book as the Oldham Corporation Act 1909.

The line from the Market Place down George Street to the Star Inn was opened on 5th December 1910 and enabled the Moorside to Hollinwood

With a ready supply of electricity available, tramway undertakings were always eager to publicise their operations by running illuminated cars around the system. On 21st July 1907 through running was re-introduced between Waterhead and Manchester and to celebrate the occasion both Oldham and Manchester ran illuminated cars along the route. The upper picture shows the Manchester car after completion in the Hyde Road workshops.

The Coronation of King George V and Queen Mary on 22nd June 1911 was commemorated by many undertakings. Oldham decorated an open top car with bunting and coloured lights which toured the system for several days. ***(both STA)***

service to be rerouted off Union Street and run up Yorkshire Street and High Street to serve the Market Place.

In December 1910 the General Manager, Mr Lewis Slattery, resigned to take up an appointment as Chief Traffic Superintendent of the London County Council Tramways. He was succeeded by Mr Joseph W Dugdale, the Manager of the neighbouring Ashton-under-Lyne Tramways, who had previously had managerial experience at Sheffield and Oxford.

With a fleet of 80 trams and the need for more to cope with the steady growth in traffic, pressure had been building up on the main depot at Wallshaw Street, despite a number of cars being housed in the old depot on Glodwick Road. So in 1910 a second depot and workshops were built on the site of the former Carriage Company's horse tram shed in Stable Street, Hollinwood, the Glodwick Road premises then becoming the base for the Permanent Way Department. The new depot, which could accommodate 40 trams, was officially opened on 18th August 1910 by the Mayor, Alderman Schofield, following which Alderman Dunkerley, the Chairman of the Tramways Committee, unveiled a marble plaque to commemorate the event.

The new trams were twelve top-covered open-balcony double-deckers from the United Electric Car Company (UECC) of Preston, successors to the Electric Railway and Tramway Carriage Works which had supplied all Oldham's previous cars. They had seats for 52 passengers and were mounted on a Preston flexible truck with electrical equipment by Siemens of Stafford. They were numbered 81-92.

Car number 89 was delivered in time for the Coronation of King George V and instead of its fleet number displayed a large crown and the legend 'King George V' on either dash for a time. Not surprisingly it became known as 'King George'. During Coronation week one of the new cars was suitably decorated and ran on various routes throughout the town.

On 21st December 1911, after replacing the short section of track that had been removed seven years before, the abandoned line along Egerton Street was reopened and the service was extended to Shaw. Once again it lost money and after only eleven months was withdrawn for good on 14th September 1912.

The Grains Bar saga

Work had now started on extending the Ripponden Road Tramway from Moorside to Grains Bar as authorised by the 1909 Act, but this had turned out to be not quite as simple as it was first thought. On 3rd August 1911 Mr Dugdale reported to the Tramways Committee on visits he had made to Bradford and Leeds to look at the new 'trackless trams' that were running there. Although Council policy was to extend the tramway, Mr Dugdale was very much in favour of running a feeder service and persuaded the Committee to visit the two cities and inspect the operation. They were obviously impressed as an approach was made to the Board of Trade to allow the extension to be provided by trolley vehicles, but the Board refused to allow it within the existing Act. The Council then decided to utilise the powers it already had under the Act to use the buses which were operating the Coppice service on weekdays to run a service on Saturdays and Sundays between Moorside and Grains Bar. This did not please the residents who complained bitterly about the noise and vibration caused by the buses and reiterated their wish for a proper and regular tram service.

So the Council capitulated and work commenced on the tramway on 23rd February 1914 using, so far as was possible, materials salvaged from the abandoned Egerton Street route. Ripponden Road at this time was little more than a cart track and in the midst of a Pennine winter had to be virtually rebuilt with foundations of boulders, scrap rails and concrete up to six feet deep to carry the weight of the trams. The job was eventually completed at a cost approaching £700,000 at today's prices for just under a mile of track, and it was opened for traffic on 4th June 1914. The Grains Bar extension was the last new tramway to be built in Oldham and although it was well-used on summer weekends and Bank Holidays when the people of Oldham escaped the smoky back streets for a day out in the fresh air, it was difficult and decidedly unpleasant to operate in the winter due its exposed moorland location. Drivers of the open-ended cars often had to contend with fog, high winds and driving snow, the route being closed for days at a time when snowdrifts blocked the tracks.

To work the extension and cater for the still growing demand on other routes seven more cars were ordered from UECC to the same design

The new depot and workshops at Hollinwood were opened in 1910 when the expanding fleet outgrew the Wallshaw Street site. In the upper view tram number 36, now fitted with a Bellamy-type top cover, stands outside the ornate front of the depot about 1913 before leaving for Lees. In the lower picture, taken about the same time, the crew of number 75, another Bellamy car, pose for the photographer at the same point but looking back towards Manchester. ***(both STA)***

as the preceding batch. Curiously they were numbered 94-100. No reference can be found to the phantom number 93 but it is possible that it was intended for another car which was never delivered. A further twelve similar cars, although with their seating increased to 58, were ordered but due to the outbreak of war were not delivered until 1915. They carried the numbers 93 and 101-111, utilising the missing number from the previous batch.

Although the number of passengers carried was steadily increasing, there were some areas of retrenchment. The abandonment of the Egerton Street line has already been mentioned but there was also the stretch of track along Union Street West which lost its service from 12th May 1913 when Oldham's first motor buses started running from the Town Hall to The Coppice.

In June of that year the long Hathershaw to Norden service, jointly operated with Rochdale Corporation, was split at Thornham Summit as Oldham did not wish to operate the open-top cars needed due to the low railway bridge in the Rochdale area. Number 3, the sole open-top bogie car was surplus to requirements and the body was used as a hut in the Permanent Way Department yard at Glodwick Road, the bogies being sold to Blackpool Corporation.

On 1st March 1912 Rochdale's trams had reached Newhey, the boundary between Milnrow UDC which leased its tracks to Rochdale and Crompton UDC, over whose lines Oldham had been operating as far as the Wren's Nest at Shaw since 1904. The gap between the two networks was a little over a mile and in 1914 Crompton, who were willing to construct the line, pressed Oldham to extend their service to link the two systems. However, the First World War intervened and powers to build the line were never sought. The area was eventually to be served by the buses of the North Western Road Car Company and it is interesting to conjecture how differently the map might have been drawn had the line been built.

Tram number 77, new in 1902, was later fitted with an extended open-vestibule top deck but is pictured at the Lees terminus in its original state. ***(STA)***

The First World War

The First World War started on 4th August 1914, bringing with it shortages and increased prices and due the high cost of steel, only the most urgent repairs were made to the track during the next five years. Another problem was the number of men enlisting in the armed forces which caused a shortage of shed staff and conductors, partly filled by the recruitment of women on a temporary basis. By January 1915 there were 60 women employees, but even so service reductions became necessary.

Oldham was never very happy with its single-deck bogie cars, which were not suited to the sharp curves on some of the routes and in any case were unnecessary as there were no low bridges in the Borough. The arrival of the twelve new double-deckers in 1915 provided the opportunity to dispose of them and all were sold to Rotherham Corporation whose operating area was bedevilled by low bridges. Some of these cars had varied careers, later moving on to Walthamstow Corporation and eventually passing with that undertaking to the London Passenger Transport Board. Later in the war more single-deckers were withdrawn and a number of open-top cars were given top-covers. By the end of the war in 1918 Oldham had a fleet of 93 trams to work a network of 24 route miles.

Mr Dugdale's reign as General Manager had been marked by an uneasy relationship with his Committee, and he eventually resigned in March 1916. He was succeeded by Mr Percy Priestly who, like Mr Wilkinson, the first General Manager, also came from a marine engineering background, but had been Manager of the Mexborough and Swinton Tramways Company for the past nine years. Mr Priestly only stayed at Oldham for two years before resigning in April 1918 to become Deputy Manager at Liverpool. The following month Mr William Chamberlain, the Borough Electrical Engineer, was appointed General Manager. Mr (later Sir William) Chamberlain would go on to have an illustrious career in the industry, moving from Oldham to Leeds and then Belfast before eventually becoming the North Western Area Traffic Commissioner on the inception of the 1930

It is 1919 and the First World War has been over for nearly a year as car number 45, now with an open vestibule top cover heads down Mumps on its way to Waterhead. Mumps railway bridge has since been demolished to make way for the new Metrolink line. ***(STA)***

Road Traffic Act and later Regional Transport Commissioner during the Second World War. But that was still some time in the future.

Towards the end of the war Chadderton UDC again raised the question of a line along Oxford Street into the district. Powers were obtained under the Oldham and Chadderton Tramways Act of 1919 with construction scheduled to begin in February 1921. However, this did not happen, Oldham looked at the possibility of both bus and trolleybus operation and again the powers lapsed.

The Post-War Years

The period immediately after the war was one of consolidation rather than innovation, catching up with the backlog of maintenance that had left the track and the rolling stock in a poor condition, the only change of any consequence being the withdrawal of the Coppice bus service and the reinstatement of the tram track along Union Street West with a service to Waterhead being operated.

Oldham's first post-war cars were delivered from English Electric during 1920-1. These were another twelve open-balcony top-covered double-deckers on Brill 21E trucks, but reverting to Dick Kerr for their electrical gear. They were numbered 4-12 and 14-16, replacing the bogie double-deckers of the same numbers dating from 1900-1 that had been withdrawn in 1915. More of the older cars were fitted with top covers. A shortage of cars resulted in the somewhat extreme example of recycling that became tram number 112, created from the body of number 3, the former 1900 bogie car which was recovered from the Glodwick Road Permanent Way yard where for several years it had been used as a platelayers' hut. It was shortened and fitted with a top cover and mounted on a new four-wheel Brill 21E truck.

Although still having open balconies, the new cars had enclosed platforms, which did not meet with universal approval from the drivers who, despite being exposed to the elements, preferred to be out in the open. One notable difference, however, was the fitting of route number boxes.

Route numbers were introduced in March 1921, replacing the coloured lights which had served since the tramway services started running in 1900. The numbers were:

1 Waterhead-Werneth-Hollinwood
2 Lees-Werneth-Hollinwood
3 Market Place-Middleton Road
4 Glodwick Circular
5 Grains Bar-Hollins Road-Hollinwood
6 Moorside-Hollins Road-Hollinwood
7 Hathershaw-Summit
8 Shaw-Werneth-Hollinwood
9 Shaw-Chadderton Road
10 Union St West-Waterhead
11 High St-Werneth-Hollinwood
12 Star Inn-Watersheddings
20 Waterhead-Werneth-Manchester

The Oldham, Ashton and Hyde Electric Tramway Company had opened its line in 1897, but the Council had refused to let it operate within the Borough, instead leasing it to the Bury, Rochdale and Oldham Steam Tramways Company and subsequently operating its own electric trams as far as Hathershaw where passengers for Ashton had to change. However, the Ashton Company's lease ran out in 1921, the tracks were linked at Hathershaw and on 2nd July a through service commenced between the Star Inn and Ashton-under-Lyne, jointly operated with the latter undertaking, which carried the number 14. The number 13 was never used on the trams and did not appear on an Oldham vehicle until the Uppermill bus service received that number in 1930 as part of Manchester's service numbering scheme.

After this things went quiet for a time, interest being focussed mainly on the continuing rebuilding of open-top cars with top covers and windscreens in the Hollinwood works. Three of these, numbers 40, 49 and 54, were also fitted with enclosed balconies, becoming Oldham's first fully enclosed cars and setting the pattern for the future. Six new fully-enclosed trams on Brill 21E trucks arrived from English Electric in 1924, numbered 17-20, 22 and 24 and again replacing withdrawn cars with the same numbers.

On 15th December 1924 a bus service started running to Hollinwood via The Coppice and once again the Union Street West line was closed, tram service 10 being curtailed at the Star Inn.

On a warm summer day passengers, including a policeman, are enjoying the sunshine on the balcony of car number 94 as it crosses the junction at the Star Inn and runs into King Street. The year is 1921 and number 94 is on its way from Hathershaw to Summit, by now showing route number 7. ***(STA)***

The 1925 Act

In 1924 Oldham Corporation decided to promote a General Act which among other things sought the following powers:

- To acquire the Middleton Electric Traction Company,
- To construct the Oxford Street tramway previously authorised by the 1919 Order,
- To purchase by agreement the tramways in Chadderton, Crompton, Lees and Royton Urban Districts which it currently leased,
- With the consent of the Minister of Transport, to operate trolleybuses on any thoroughfare in the Borough and the above four districts where it already ran trams and
- To operate motor omnibuses up to five miles beyond its boundaries with the consent of the Local Authority concerned.

Rochdale Corporation objected to the first clause and as a result Oldham agreed to limit its proposed operation to the line through Chadderton to Middleton and on to Rhodes where it would meet Manchester's trams. With this assurance Rochdale withdrew its objection and on 7th August 1925 the Bill received the Royal Assent becoming the Oldham Corporation Act 1925.

The Middleton Electric Traction Company had operated on a 21-year lease from Chadderton, Middleton and Rochdale that had already expired on 15th December 1923 and had been extended temporarily pending discussions on its future. Eventually, agreement was reached and the Company was purchased by Manchester, Rochdale and Oldham Corporations on 15th June 1925. Oldham's share was the portion of the tracks within Chadderton and it took over the operation from 9th August, running through from Oldham to Middleton. Subsequently, under the provisions of the 1925 Act, it purchased the stretch of line within Chadderton as far as the Middleton boundary at Mills Hill.

As part of the purchase Oldham acquired eight single-deck single-truck cars that had originated with the Oldham, Ashton and Hyde Company, numbering them 113 to 120, which they continued to use on the service due to the low height of the railway bridge at Mills Hill.

The Middleton Electric Traction Company was taken over by Manchester, Rochdale and Oldham Corporations on 15th June 1925 and Oldham started running between the Market Place and Middleton from 9th August. For the time being the existing Middleton cars were used on the service due to the low bridge at Mills Hill. The two upper pictures show former Middleton car number 115 passing Chadderton Cemetery soon after Oldham took over the operation and heavily-loaded car number 119 crossing Rochdale Road on the last few yards of its journey from Middleton to the Market Place, while below an unidentified former MET car, now displaying the Oldham Coat of Arms, stands at Mills Hill Bridge on a journey from the Market Place to Middleton. The railway embankment carrying the LMS railway line from Manchester to Leeds can be seen in the background. ***(all STA)***

Trolleybuses

A through tram service had been running between Oldham and Ashton-under-Lyne since 1921. However, the condition of the track in Ashton, inherited from the former BET-owned Oldham, Ashton and Hyde Company, was giving cause for concern, but the cost of renewal was prohibitive. Looking for a cheaper alternative Ashton had promoted its own Bill, which became the Ashton-under-Lyne Corporation Act 1924 containing powers to run trolleybuses and the passing of Oldham's Act enabled through running between Oldham and Ashton to continue.

Oldham purchased two trolleybuses identical to those of Ashton and garaged them in the now disused Copster Hill tram shed. Numbered 1 and 2, they were Railless LFT30 single-deckers with a 34-seat centre-entrance body by Short Brothers of Rochester.

After a ceremonial opening during which civic dignitaries of both towns rode along the route, the public service started on 26th August 1925, some two weeks after the Act came into force. But there were problems right from the start, mainly due to the buses sharing the same positive wire as the trams, and the noise and vibration caused by the solid-tyres on granite setts led to numerous complaints by frontagers. The service was short-lived and on 2nd April 1926 it was split at Hathershaw with Oldham replacing its portion with motor buses between Hathershaw and Summit, although trams were still used on some peak hour workings. The two trolleybuses remained in the Copster Hill shed until they were eventually sold to Ashton for spares.

Once again the powers to build the tramway along Oxford Street were allowed to lapse and buses were used instead.

The writing on the wall

In April 1925 Mr Chamberlain resigned to become General Manager of Leeds Corporation Tramways. His replacement as Oldham's General Manager was Mr Clement Jackson. Mr Jackson was born in Huddersfield and had been Works Superintendent at Sheffield Corporation Tramways before the war, during which he attained the rank of Captain and was awarded the Military Cross. He returned to Sheffield in 1918 and became General Manager of Keighley Corporation Tramways in 1922.

Posed outside the Short Brothers factory, trolleybus number 2 was one of a pair of short-lived Railless vehicles identical to those purchased by Ashton-under-Lyne at the same time. ***(STA)***

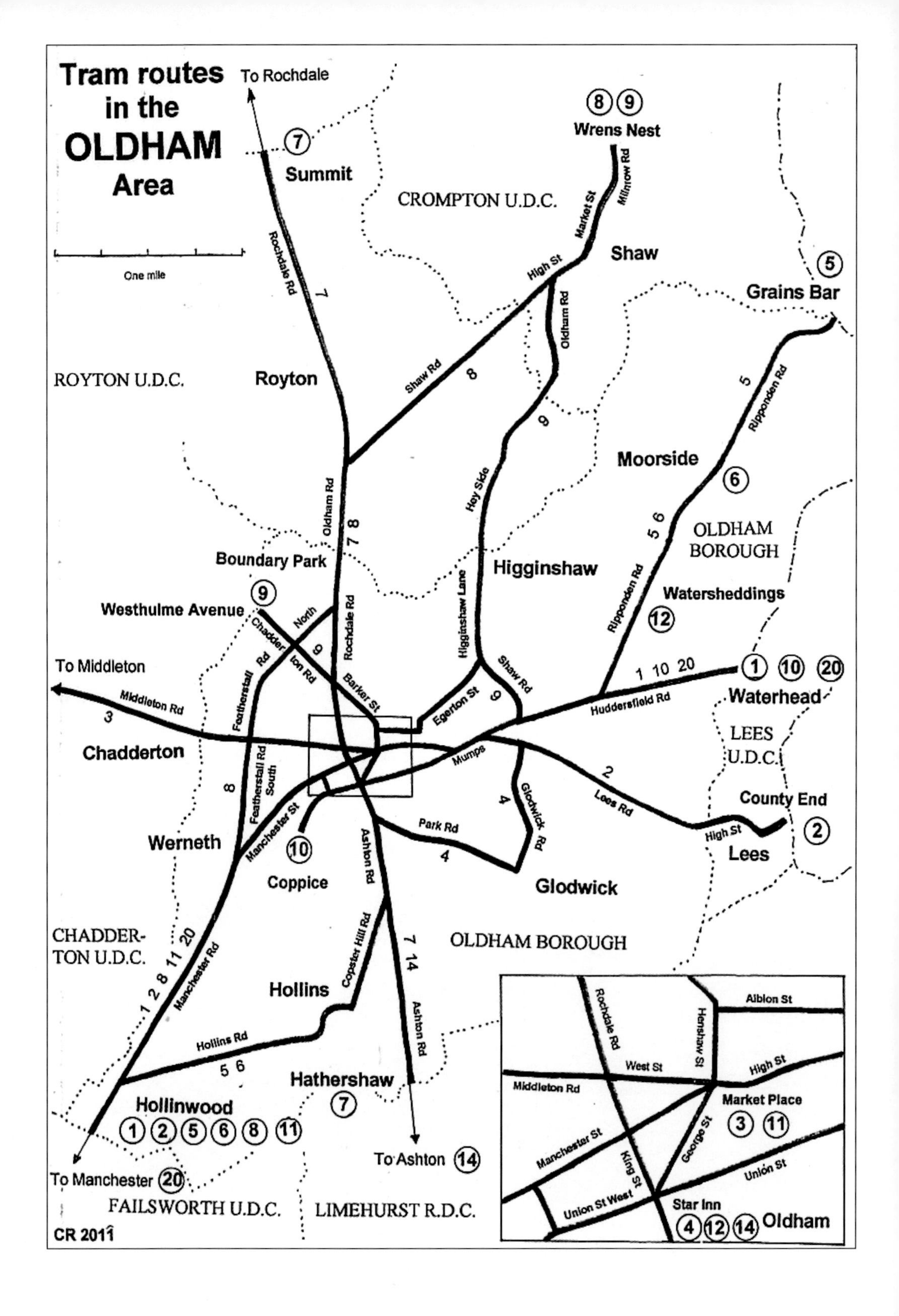

Tram routes in the OLDHAM Area
To Rochdale
One mile
7 Summit
CROMPTON U.D.C.
8 9 Wrens Nest
Milnrow Rd
Market St
High St
Shaw
Rochdale Rd
7
Oldham Rd
5 Grains Bar
ROYTON U.D.C.
Royton
Shaw Rd
8
9
Ripponden Rd
5
Moorside
6
Hey Side
Oldham Rd
7 8
56
OLDHAM BOROUGH
Boundary Park
Higginshaw
Ripponden Rd
Watersheddings
12
9
Westhulme Avenue
North
Chadderton Rd
Rochdale Rd
Higginshaw Lane
Shaw Rd
1 10 20
1 10 20
Waterhead
To Middleton
Middleton Rd
3
Featherstall Rd
9
Barker St
Egerton St
9
Huddersfield Rd
LEES U.D.C.
Chadderton
Featherstall Rd South
Mumps
2
8
Manchester St
Glodwick Rd
4
Lees Rd
County End
High St
2
Werneth
10
Ashton Rd
Park Rd
4
Lees
Coppice
Glodwick
CHADDER-TON U.D.C.
1 2 8 11 20
Manchester Rd
Copster Hill Rd
7 14
OLDHAM BOROUGH
Hollins
Ashton Rd
Hollins Rd
5 6
Hathershaw
7
Hollinwood
1 2 5 6 8 11
To Ashton 14
To Manchester 20
FAILSWORTH U.D.C.
LIMEHURST R.D.C.
CR 2011
Rochdale Rd
Henshaw St
Albion St
West St
High St
Middleton Rd
Market Place
3 11
Manchester St
King St
George St
Union St
Union St West
Star Inn
4 12 14 Oldham

Number 40, originally an open-top car new in 1902, had been heavily rebuilt to the latest standards by the time this photograph was taken in 1927, showing it climbing up Manchester Street on its way to Lees. ***(MMT)***

A further twelve new cars entered service during 1925. These were built by English Electric on the standard Preston 21E truck with Dick Kerr electrical gear and were fully enclosed. They were numbered 121-32, the highest number reached, and brought the fleet up to a peak strength of 125 cars. Despite this there were signs that the electric tram was beginning to lose its supremacy over other forms of transport. The line along Union Street West had already been replaced by a bus service and now the Hathershaw to Summit route had also been turned over to motor bus operation.

Despite the failure of the original vehicles, Oldham and Ashton were still discussing the use of more modern trolleybuses on the route. The Oxford Street line had been finally laid to rest and during the next couple of years more motor bus services were introduced running partly over sections of the tram network. As yet there was no talk of abandoning the tramways, but the twelve new trams were to be the last purchased by Oldham.

Then, in 1928, Mr Jackson recommended the conversion of the Lees Road route to motor buses due to the worn condition of the track. The Tramways Committee agreed the proposal but, as not enough new buses were available due to increasing traffic elsewhere, the unusual decision was taken to re-introduce trams on the Hathershaw-Summit service for a temporary period. The latter change took place on 1st May 1928, buses starting running along Lees Road the following day.

The Ripponden Road route was the next to go, buses taking over on 24th December, the last new section of track built in the Borough from Moorside up to Grains Bar being almost the first to go after only 14 years of operation, although the relatively new rails were re-used elsewhere on the system. The section of line in Ripponden Road as far as Watersheddings was retained for a short time for special cars to matches at Oldham Rugby League Club's ground.

Mr Jackson resigned in November 1929 to take up the post of General Manager at Plymouth and was replaced by the Works Superintendent Mr John Frederick Richards.

The late 1920s and early 1930s was a turbulent time with its trade depression, mass unemployment and political unrest which eventually culminated in the Second World War. With its reliance on heavy industry Oldham was hit particularly badly and the rise in unemployment reduced passenger journeys and led to a drop in revenue. To trim the costs frequencies were reduced, fares increased and employees working hours were cut and by 1933 the undertaking was making a small profit.

The former Middleton cars, which were the

oldest in the fleet, were beginning to feel their age and getting beyond economic repair and two of the remaining open-top cars, 43 and 47, were rebuilt as single-deckers. However, the bridge at Mills Hill was rebuilt during 1934 so that double-deck cars could run through to Middleton and all the remaining single-deck cars were withdrawn and scrapped.

Decline and fall

In 1934 it was decided to abandon the remaining tram routes and replace them with buses, mainly because of the proposed rebuilding of the Market Place and the large proportion of single track with passing loops in narrow streets which slowed down the service.

The first conversions came on 11th June 1935 when services 3 (Market Place-Middleton) and 9 (Chadderton Road-Market Place-Shaw) went over to motor bus operation and six months later on 21st December 12 (Market Place-Hollinwood via Hollins) followed. These changes resulted in the withdrawal of 39 cars, the majority of which were dismantled in Glodwick Road yard.

Next to go were 4 (Glodwick Circular), 7 (Hathershaw-Star Inn-Summit) and peak hour 10 (Star Inn-Waterhead) on 6th November 1937. The resulting withdrawal and breaking up of a further 25 cars meant that there was room for all the remaining cars in the Wallshaw Street depot, so the Hollinwood depot and works were closed in May 1938.

This left just two routes remaining, 8 (Shaw-Royton-Hollinwood) and the main line, 20 (Waterhead-Market Place-Hollinwood-Manchester) which were scheduled for conversion in September 1939. However, this was not to be. On 1st September German tanks rolled into Poland and two days later Britain declared war on Germany. The Second World War had begun.

Wartime and after

The track on much of the Shaw route was in poor condition and despite fuel shortages it was decided to go along with the conversion of service 8, buses taking over on 2nd December leaving only 27 cars remaining. The withdrawn cars were not broken up at Glodwick Road, but were sent down to Manchester instead.

Now only service 20 was still operated by trams. Here the situation was different as the track between Oldham and Hollinwood had only been re-laid comparatively recently and was in good condition. Oldham had been talking with Manchester about using trolleybuses for the conversion of the route, which Manchester had been keen to do as much of the route along Oldham Road was already wired for existing services. However, Oldham were wary of a repeat of the 1926 fiasco and in the end it had been decided not to go ahead with the idea.

So service 20 became the last tram route. Oldham worked it with their twelve newest cars of the 1926 batch, numbers 121-32, while Manchester invariably turned out their lightweight Pullman cars dating from 1930-32 which were fitted with track brakes. Manchester's big bogie cars never worked beyond Hollinwood. The trams soldiered on throughout the six years of the war as the track and electrical equipment crumbled around them. Things got so bad that in 1942 a journalist on the *Oldham Chronicle* wrote that 'a ride down Manchester Street on a tramcar bears a distinct resemblance to being on board ship during a gale'.

Mr Richards died on 4th October 1943. He was succeeded as General Manager by Mr Cyril Percy Paige who held a similar position with Bury Corporation Tramways.

On 9th May 1945 the war ended in Europe and a year later on 3rd August 1946 car number 4 became Oldham's last tram to run in service. Repainted and decorated for the occasion it worked throughout the afternoon and finally ran behind the last service car from the Town Hall to Hollinwood, then to Waterhead and back to depot. On the last leg it was driven by the Mayor of Oldham, Alderman Marran and carried Members of the Council, the officers of the Tramways Department and guests.

Tramways were no more. Of the remaining cars six, numbers 17, 18, 24, 122, 125 and 128, were sold to the Gateshead and District Tramways, the rest being broken up. Twenty of the bodies were sold to the Middleton Towers Holiday Camp near Morecambe for use as chalets, the trucks and motors being exported to Calcutta for further use. Wallshaw Street remains in use as a depot for First Group but otherwise nothing remains of the tramway system that served Oldham for 46 years.

The long Manchester to Waterhead route was jointly operated with Manchester Corporation. Oldham only had four-wheel cars and the inter-running agreement stipulated that Manchester also should only use four-wheel cars to prevent them getting more than their share of revenue. In later years Manchester turned out Stewart Pilcher's lightweight Pullman cars, fitted with magnetic track brakes to work in Oldham. Manchester car number 287, new in September 1931, is pictured (upper) dropping down High Street on its way to Waterhead. ***(STA)***

In 1920, to address a shortage of cars the body of number 3, which had been used as a platelayers hut in the Glodwick Road depot yard for the past five years, was resurrected and placed on a new Brill 21E truck. Originally a six-bay lower deck with reversed stairs, it was shortened, rebuilt with five windows and direct stairs and fitted with a four-window open-balcony top. It was given the number 112 and in this form ran for a further 19 years. Number 112 is seen (middle) leaving the Wallshaw Street workshops shortly before its withdrawal. ***(STA)***

Oldham's last trams were a batch of ten delivered in 1926. Car number 124, photographed (lower) at the Market Place in 1937, shows the final stage in the evolution of the English Electric tramcar on the Brill 21E truck. It operated through the Second World War and was withdrawn with the conversion of service 20 to motor buses in 1946. ***(STA)***

The last day of tramway operation in Oldham was 3rd August 1946. Tram number 4 of the 1920 batch was decorated for the occasion and after running between Hollinwood and Waterhead throughout the afternoon and evening it followed the last service car on its final journey. Number 4 is seen at Waterhead during the afternoon and later back in the depot having been driven on the last leg by the Mayor of Oldham, Alderman Marran. ***(both STA)***

THE TRAM FLEET

Year	Fleet Nos	Type	Trucks	Body
1900	1	Single-deck 4-wheel	Brill 21E	ERTCW
1900	2	Open-top 4-wheel	Brill 21E	ERTCW
1900	3	Open-top bogie	Brill 22E	ERTCW
1900	4	Single-deck bogie	Brill 27G	ERTCW
1901	5-16	Single-deck bogie	Brill 27G	ERTCW
1902	17-26	Single-deck 4-wheel	Brill 21E	ERTCW
1902	27-42	Open-top 4-wheel	Brill 21E	ERTCW
1902	43-67	Open top 4-wheel	Brill 21E	ERTCW
1903	68-80	Open-top 4-wheel	Brill 21E	ERTCW
1911	81-92	Balcony 4-wheel	Preston	UEC
1913	94-100	Balcony 4-wheel	Preston	UEC
1915	93, 101-111	Balcony 4-wheel	Preston 21E	UEC
1921	4-12, 14-16	Balcony 4-wheel	Preston 21E	EE
1921	112	Balcony 4-wheel	Brill 21E	Oldham
1924	17-20, 22, 24	Enclosed 4-wheel	Preston 21E	EE
1925	113-120	Single-deck 4-wheel	Peckham	Brush
1926	121-132	Enclosed 4-wheel	Preston 21E	EE

112 was built by Oldham Corporation using the shortened body of car 3

113-120 came from the Middleton Electric Traction Company in 1925 and were new to the Oldham, Ashton and Hyde Company in 1899.

Wallshaw Street depot about 1927. ***(STA)***

4 – *EARLY BUSES*

A faltering start

By 1912, with the exception of the mile or so beyond Moorside, the tramway network was now complete and all the major roads in the Borough were covered by frequent services of modern electric cars. However, infilling was taking place, one such area being the Coppice, a growing well-to-do suburb situated to the south of the town between Manchester Road and Ashton Road beyond the terminus of the Union Street West tram line.

Pressure was exerted on the Council by the influential residents of the Coppice to provide some form of service. However, due to the network of narrow residential roads in the area an extension of the tram service would have been difficult and prohibitively expensive, so the Tramways Committee decided to experiment with motor buses. Back in 1907 the Committee had looked at the possibility of using buses as a feeder service from Grains Bar to the trams at Moorside and had found them noisy and unreliable to run, but six years had passed and the product had improved.

In September 1912 the Committee noted that the 'Stephen Pilling' (sic) petrol-driven omnibus was running in London and Sheffield and it was suggested that, if it was suitable, a similar type of vehicle might be used to provide a service for the Coppice. Consequently the Mayor and the General Manager travelled to London to inspect one. Mr Dugdale recommended the purchase of three of the buses but, not for the first time, the Committee over-ruled their General Manager and decided to purchase only two. In the January a Daimler bus was borrowed from the manufacturer and trials were run around the streets of the Coppice and also, perhaps with an eye to the future, on the steeply graded two miles of road between Grains Bar and Denshaw. The trial was said to be very satisfactory, but nothing more came of it.

The buses arrived and were garaged in the Copster Hill depot, the sand drier being removed to Glodwick Road to make room. On 12th May 1913 they began working a service from the Town Hall along Clegg Street, Union Street, Union Street West, Werneth Hall Road, Coppice Street, Wellington Road and Windsor Road to College Road on weekdays, a distance of just under a mile, in part replacing the tram route which was then cut back to the Star Inn. They carried open-top bodies with 16 inward facing seats inside and

An early picture of the *"Stephen Pillings"*. Oldham's first buses were these two Tilling-Stevens petrol-electrics posed here with their crews in their very smart dark blue and white livery. ***(STA)***

18 slatted wooden garden seats on top and were painted in the same blue and cream livery that had been used on the first batch of trams and which was to become standard for the next few years.

All new buses would be registered in the town carrying the BU prefix which had been allocated to Oldham County Borough Council in the early days of motoring and the newcomers were registered BU 401 and BU 402. Belatedly, accepting that a spare vehicle was needed to cover breakdowns, the Committee agreed to purchase a third identical bus. It was registered BU11, a number previously carried by a scrapped lorry. In common with other vehicles of the time the buses had solid tyres which gave rise to numerous complaints of noise and vibration on the cobbled roads of the period. The route was altered on several occasions over the years to placate indignant householders who wanted the service as long as it didn't pass their front doors.

The buses were also used on Saturdays and Sundays to provide a service between Moorside and Grains Bar. However, this proved unpopular with both groups as the Grains Bar passengers wanted a service during the week while the residents of the Coppice wanted to get into town to shop on Saturdays. A petition was received from the residents of Moorside complaining of the inconvenience caused by, 'The assemblage of passengers waiting to board the buses at Moorside.' The Moorside trams were extended to Grains Bar on 4th June 1914 and the shuttle was withdrawn, the bus then being used to provide a further shuttle from Grains Bar to Denshaw commencing on 31st August. As this was outside the Borough, special permission had to be obtained from Saddleworth District and the West Riding County Council.

As well as granting the Council powers to operate buses, the Oldham Corporation Act of 1909 had also included a new section of tramway into Chadderton along Oxford Street. This of course never materialised and in June 1914 Chadderton Council wrote to Oldham requesting that, 'Some provision be made for the large number of residents and workpeople in their district which were not served by tramways or other vehicular service and whether it could consider providing a motor bus service along Oxford Street to Werneth Fire Station.' Conveniently forgetting that it was already running a bus service in the West Riding of Yorkshire, Oldham pointed out that the Act prevented it operating outside its own area but agreed to approach the Board of Trade to sanction it. Whether or not it ever did is not recorded, but Oldham did not operate buses in Chadderton for another eleven years.

On 10th August 1915 the town terminus of the Coppice route was altered from the Town Hall to the General Post Office on Union Street. Now, due to the escalation of fuel prices because of the war, costs were becoming too great; the bus services were running at a loss and a halfpenny increase on the longer fares was considered but not agreed. In April 1916 it was decided to withdraw the service and the three buses were offered to Rotherham Corporation for £750 each. Rotherham was not willing to pay this and was then asked to make an offer, as were Tilling-Stevens, the original suppliers, but both declined. The buses soldiered on for a while, but the Coppice route was temporarily suspended in August 1916 due to a shortage of petrol and the Denshaw service was withdrawn on the 27th of the month. In 1917 the service to the Coppice was reduced to a one-bus operation and to provide sufficient capacity a second hand 26-seat bus body was purchased and fitted to the chassis of BU 401. The other two buses were now surplus to requirements and were sold to Warrington Corporation for an undisclosed price. BU 401 was later converted to run on consumer gas carried in a bag on the roof, a move that presaged a similar policy during the Second World War that was never really satisfactory.

Since it was impossible to operate the service without spare coverage, a battery powered Commercial Truck Co. chassis was acquired from the Electromobile Company of Leeds in February 1918 and was fitted with the Tilling-Stevens body originally on BU 401 which had lain unused in the Copster Hill garage for over a year. The complete vehicle was then re-registered BU 69. However, it was underpowered for the hilly nature of the route and the batteries were prone to running flat. After the bus was regularly towed back to depot it was eventually decided to abandon bus operation altogether and the Coppice service was withdrawn on 13th September 1919. Subsequently, BU 69 was sold to Belgrave Mills who used it for staff transport until August 1920 when it was replaced by TB 2554, a former Leyland demonstrator which, by a twist of fate, was to come into the Oldham fleet in 1925.

The Union Street West tram service was then reinstated and the Council did not operate motor buses again for another five years.

Holt and North Western

Although Oldham had suffered difficulties with its first bus services, largely it has to be said as a result of wartime conditions, progress with motor buses was gathering momentum elsewhere. During 1923 Holt Bros (Rochdale) Ltd, who were later to become much better known as Yelloway Motor Services, introduced a number of routes in Shaw and Saddleworth.

In May of that year they started a service linking the tram termini at Grains Bar and County End, Lees via Delph, Uppermill and Grasscroft, but within a short while altered the route to terminate instead at Waterhead. At the same time a long circuitous route was introduced between High Crompton and Uppermill via Shaw, Newhey, Denshaw and Delph. There was also a short-lived service between Denshaw and Mytholmroyd near Halifax via Ripponden and Sowerby Bridge.

Then in 1924 competition arrived in the shape of the North Western Road Car Company. North Western had been formed the previous year out of the British Automobile Traction Company's Macclesfield and Peak District area with the injection of an equal amount of capital by Thomas Tilling Limited. A new depot was opened at Charles Street, Stockport and the Company used this as a springboard to expand north and east around the Manchester conurbation. In March 1924 both Holt and North Western applied to Oldham for licences to run services from Oldham to Uppermill both via Scouthead and Delph and via Lees and Grasscroft. After much discussion Oldham granted licences to North Western subject to protecting their local tram services by charging a minimum fare double that of the tram within the Oldham operating area. Holt's application was refused, but he continued to run illegally until threatened with court action when he withdrew from the routes. North Western's buses were garaged in a small depot in Slater Street near the town centre off Manchester Street and the services started from Rock Street behind the Parish Church. The terminus was later moved to the GPO on Greaves Street. The Corporation took part in the operation from 1929 as a consequence of the changes in the express services.

Crompton District Council was also unhappy with Holt's somewhat erratic performance in their area. By now North Western had gained a reputation for professional and efficient operation and when the Company applied for two services between Delph and Rochdale (one via Grains Bar, Shaw and High Crompton and the other via Denshaw and Newhey), they quickly granted it the necessary licences. However, neither Rochdale nor Milnrow Councils would agree to the services running over their tram routes and after some delay a revised application was made for two overlapping routes from Newhey to the Rochdale boundary at Broad Lane via Shaw and High Crompton and from Delph to High Crompton via Denshaw, Newhey and Shaw, duplicating Oldham's trams between the Wren's Nest and Shaw town centre.

Oldham naturally objected but, after agreeing to charge a higher minimum fare over this section, the new services, by now extended from Delph to Uppermill, came into operation in October 1924. North Western and Rochdale then entered into a joint running agreement for a revised service between Rochdale and Shaw which commenced on 17th August 1927. The company later extended its workings to Piethorn but when the route was diverted in Shaw to serve new housing at Bank House, the North Western workings on service 2 were extended up Huddersfield Road to Peppermint Bridge in their place. The Uppermill to High Crompton service was cut back to Newhey and extended beyond Uppermill to Friezland, an infrequent service which ran for many years before withdrawal in 1969. Thirty years later three round trips were run between Friezland and Rochdale on two days a week for a number of years, finally achieving North Western's ambitions of some 70 years earlier, long after the company itself had vanished from the scene.

With North Western now taking most of his passengers Holt withdrew from bus operation totally during 1925 to concentrate on building up his charabanc business. North Western went on to consolidate its operations and built up a network of services in Saddleworth and Crompton, much of which was later to be run jointly with Oldham and eventually integrated with their operation in PTE days, the whole area becoming part of an enlarged Oldham Borough under the 1973 Local

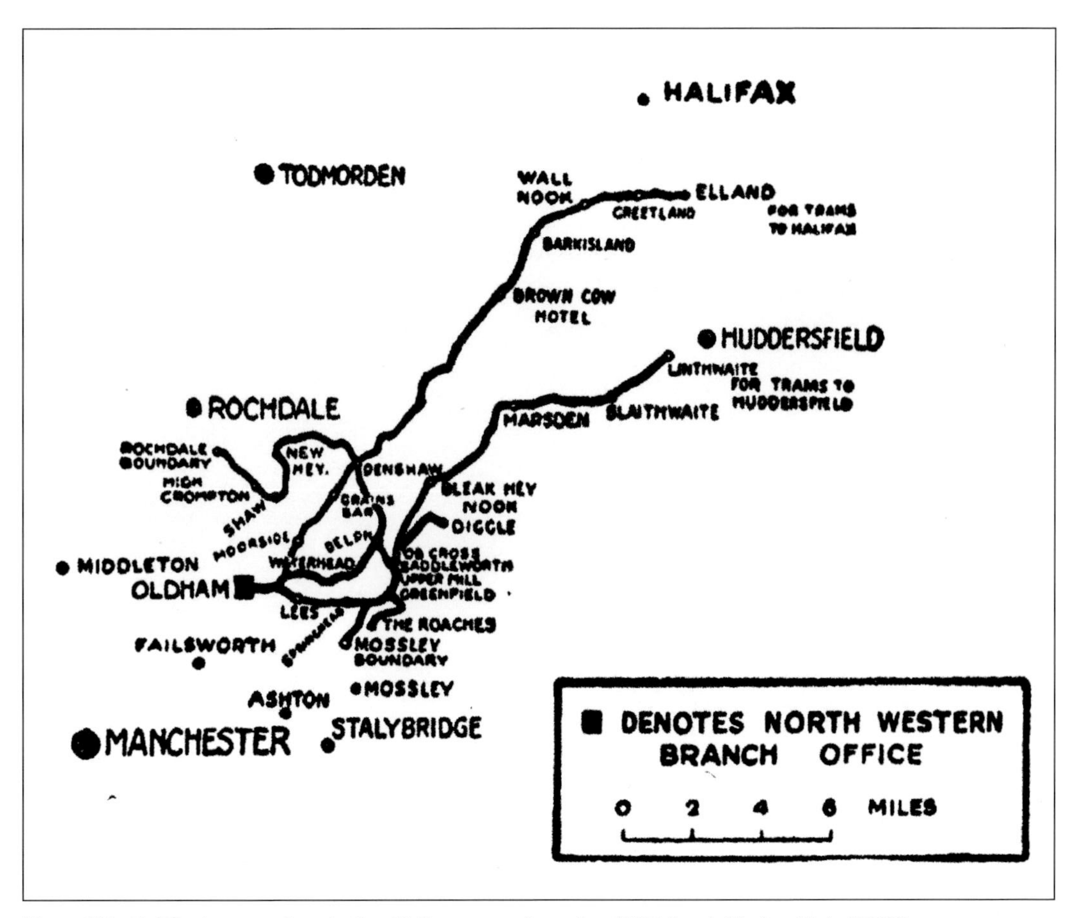

Map of North Western services in the Oldham area from the 1925 timetable booklet. ***(DBC)***

Government Act.

Oldham, meanwhile, was having tentative discussions with Halifax, Huddersfield, Todmorden, Ashton-under-Lyne and Rochdale Corporations and the Stalybridge, Hyde, Mossley and Dukinfield Tramways and Electricity Board, with a view to operating bus services between the industrial areas of Lancashire and Yorkshire '*on the basis of joint operation and responsibility.*' The two proposed services in which Oldham was interested were to Halifax via Denshaw and Ripponden and to Huddersfield via Delph and Marsden. Known as the Joint Control Committee, the scheme never got off the ground, but on 8th April 1925 North Western introduced a service from Oldham to the Huddersfield boundary at Linthwaite via Uppermill and Marsden, Huddersfield Council refusing the company permission to operate within the Borough boundaries in order to protect its own local tram route. The service ran until 28th March 1929 when it was incorporated into a Manchester to Huddersfield route, eventually to become part of the Liverpool to Newcastle service. On 3rd December 1932 a service was introduced between Oldham and Huddersfield via Scouthead and Delph which ran for many years as its service 160.

At this point mention should be made of Hanson's service between Huddersfield and Oldham. Joseph Hanson and Sons first ran buses in the Huddersfield area in the early 1920s and became Hanson's Buses Ltd in 1935.They started running their red buses on a service between Oldham and Huddersfield via Uppermill and Marsden on 21st March 1930. The operation was sold to Huddersfield Corporation in 1969 as its service 65 and passed to the West Yorkshire PTE on 1st April 1974. First Manchester now runs an hourly service between Manchester and Huddersfield over a similar route.

Above.
Hanson's number 59 was an AEC Regal with Brush 32-seat body dating from 1933. Here it poses for an official photograph somewhere on the rain-swept Pennines, its indicators set for the Oldham route. It received a Burlingham body in 1941 and was withdrawn in 1948.

Left.
When bus operation was revived in 1924 Oldham's first buses were five Leyland C9 24-seat single-deckers for the Coppice route. These were joined a year later by four slightly longer C7 models seating 28 for the Broadway route, One of the latter batch is pictured in the Leyland factory before receiving its fleet number and registration plates. ***(both STA)***

A new beginning

During the early 1920s Oldham Corporation found itself in a dilemma. With new post-war housing springing up beyond the existing tram routes there was a growing need to provide some form of service and the Council was in a position common to other towns and cities across the country at that time. The new housing was at a much lower density than previously and the potential revenue would not sustain the investment needed to build new tramways. Thoughts therefore turned again to motorbuses.

The first of these routes was basically a re-introduction of the original service to the Coppice, but extended at both ends to run between Mumps and Hollinwood. The actual origin of the name Mumps which nowadays refers both to a street and a former railway station is shrouded in mystery but it may derive from the word 'Mumpers', a local name for the beggars and other vagabonds who once inhabited the area.

To run the service five driver-operated Leyland C9 normal control 24-seat single-deckers were acquired and numbered 1-5. They were a great improvement on the earlier buses and were fitted with pneumatic tyres and gave a reliable service for up to ten years. They were garaged in the former steam tram shed at Royton which was reopened for the purpose and went into service on 15th December 1924. However, following a complaint from the LMS Railway that the Hollinwood terminus in Station Street was on their property, the service was cut back to the junction of Chapel Road and Manchester Road on 16th March 1925, the time saved conveniently allowing the Corporation to accede to a request for a service up Greenacres Road to a terminus at Greenacres Cemetery.

Early in 1925, Oldham was discussing with Chadderton and Royton District Councils how best to serve the new arterial road between Failsworth and Royton which was to due to open shortly. Meanwhile Manchester informed Oldham that it had applied to run buses along the road but if Oldham were to run along the route then it would withdraw its operation. This caused a few ripples as Oldham, who already ran the trams in the surrounding districts, considered Chadderton and Royton to be their operating area. So Oldham acted swiftly, starting a service on 28th February from the top of Garforth Street, a few yards from the Chadderton Road tram terminus, along Burnley Lane and the new road by then named Broadway, to the Manchester boundary at Moston Lane East. At this time Oldham had no powers to operate buses outside the Borough, but it ran with Chadderton's tacit agreement. Five months later on 25th July, three days after the passing of the 1925 Bill that made it legal, the service was re-routed in Chadderton and extended northwards to Royton town centre and on 29th August was extended again, this time at the other end along Moston Lane East, Hale Lane and Oldham Road to Failsworth Pole. Ironically, the whole length of Moston Lane East lay within the City of Manchester but it was not to be served by Manchester's own buses for another 20 years, by which time Oldham operation had long ceased.

With two services now running and others planned there was a need to identify them to the public and, as the tram routes were numbered, it was decided to use letters instead. Consequently, the service between Greenacres and Chapel Road became A, while the Broadway route became B. Four more new buses were ordered and arrived in May 1925. Numbered 6-9, these were Leyland C7s, a longer version of the C9 with four more seats.

For some time Chadderton had been pressing for a service linking the southern part of the District with the Town Hall and on 1st August 1925 Oldham introduced service C between Clegg Street railway station and Middleton Junction via Middleton Road, Lansdowne Road, Fields New Road, Thompson Lane, Eaves Lane, Foxdenton Lane and Grimshaw Lane, the low bridge at Middleton Junction station ensuring that single-deck buses were always used on this service and its successors. From 29th September 1926 the town terminus was moved from Clegg Street to the Star Inn.

During 1925 there was some discussion in Council on the question of using top-covered double-deckers on further proposed bus services. Opinion was divided on their safety due to their greater height and higher centre of gravity, and deputations from the Tramways Committee visited Sheffield to inspect AEC buses of that type operating there. They also visited Nottingham to inspect their Dennis double-deckers and subsequently an order was placed for seven AEC 507 chassis with 52-seat bodies by Charles

Number 12 (BU 3993) was one of Oldham's first order for double-deckers. Delivered in 1925 it was an AEC 507 model with its body coming from Charles H Roe, the Leeds coachbuilder which would supply Oldham with over 400 bus bodies over the next 46 years. The lower picture shows the Spartan layout of the upper deck. ***(both STA)***

H Roe of Leeds, thus beginning Oldham's long association with that bodybuilder.

For the past five years Belgrave Mill had been running services from its Honeywell Lane premises at Hathershaw to the Star Inn and from Rhodes Bank to Chadderton (Wash Brook) via Manchester Street and Oxford Street, mainly for its own employees. The services were acquired by the Corporation during 1925, and as previously mentioned, TD 2554, an elderly open-top Leyland double-decker came with them. Oldham took over the service from 20th August 1925 designating it D and finally running along roads for which tramway powers had twice been granted and twice allowed to lapse. Initially, it continued to be operated by the former Belgrave Mill bus which became number 10 in the fleet, although it was traded in against an eighth AEC and was withdrawn when the first of the new buses arrived shortly afterwards.

The growing network

The new buses were numbered 10-17 and came with solid tyres, but were eventually converted to pneumatics. Although the top deck was covered in, they had an open staircase and rear platform. The arrival of these eight buses during 1925 released an equivalent number of single-deckers which could be used for new services.

The first of these to be considered was from the Town Hall to Upper Mossley following the Lees Road tram route as far as County End then via Springhead and Grotton to Brookbottom where it would connect with the Ashton-under-Lyne Corporation and SHMD services to Ashton and Stalybridge respectively. Despite objections from North Western and the refusal by Saddleworth Urban District Council to grant a licence, the new service E started on 23rd January 1926, jointly operated with the SHMD Board.

SHMD was also in dispute with North Western and a hearing was held in Oldham Town Hall on 23rd March 1926 when the Ministry of Transport Inspector took the unusual step of adjourning the proceedings and 'inviting' the three parties to meet under a Ministry chairman and reach an agreement which would make a Ministry of Transport ruling unnecessary. Eventually, on 19th July 1927 a formal agreement was signed between Oldham Corporation, the Stalybridge, Hyde, Mossley and Dukinfield Transport Board and the North Western Road Car Company designating their operational boundaries and setting out conditions for joint working. So far as Oldham was concerned the districts of Saddleworth and Crompton were acknowledged as North Western territory, although Oldham's existing rights in those areas were to be safeguarded. Oldham's consent would be needed within the Borough, but not 'within territory more than three miles south of a horizontal line drawn through Oldham Town Hall.' It was this latter clause that later allowed North Western to operate into Woodhouses.

With 17 buses now in service and more on order, the old steam tramway shed at Royton was becoming too cramped, and was in any case inconvenient as it was located two miles north of the town centre and away from the routes it served. The site of the old Croft Bank Mill on Lees Road was considered but the price was too high and eventually the Corporation bought a plot of land at the top of Henshaw Street less than half a mile from the Market Place. The tender for constructing the depot went to the local firm of S and J Smethurst and the new building became operational on 10th October 1926, the official opening taking place eleven days later. But the fleet was growing and within three years it had to be extended, Tramways Committee Chairman Alderman Cheetham formally opening the enlarged premises on 12th June 1929.

Three more buses, six-wheel Guy BX-type double-deckers with 54-seat top-covered bodies again by Roe, were delivered in November 1926 and carried the numbers 18-20. The BX chassis, with its long bonnet and normal-control layout, was primarily intended to take a single-deck body and was an unusual choice for double-deckers. With the driving cab set back and partitioned off from the lower saloon, nearside visibility was poor and the buses were never popular with their drivers. After withdrawal two of them, numbers 18 and 20, survived for many years as pavilions at Oldham Cricket Club. These unorthodox vehicles were the only ones of their kind to run in Oldham and were quickly followed by a further seven normal-control Guys numbered 21-27, this time with more conventional 32-seat single-deck bodies built by Guy themselves. These were the BKX model, fitted with a Daimler engine incorporating American-designed Knight sleeve valves.

This influx of new vehicles enabled additional services to be operated. First, on New Years Day 1927 came route G which started from the Town Hall and ran along Waterloo Street to Glodwick, then followed Abbey Hills Road as far as Manor Road. Four weeks later on 28th January service D was extended the short distance from Wash Brook to Coalshaw Green, penetrating further into Chadderton. Then on 6th April service A was extended from its terminus at Greenacres Cemetery to Waterhead and up the hill through Austerlands to Scouthead. Saddleworth District Council then asked for the route to be extended again along Platting Lane to Lydgate then back through Lees to Oldham as a circular service. Oldham initially turned down the request but later agreed and obtained powers, but the option was never taken up and with the extension of the express service to Scouthead the route was cut back first to Yew Crescent on 8th March 1928 and finally to its original terminus at Greenacres Cemetery on 14th October 1929.

Also on 6th April 1927 another new service was introduced between Shaw and Middleton, via Higher Crompton, Thornham Road, Dogford Road, Royton town centre, Street Bridge and Haigh Lane to Mills Hill and then avoiding the tram route by diverting along Hilton Fold Lane, Green Lane and Boarshaw Road to serve Middleton's Boarshaw estate. Service F, as it became, was initially operated by single-deck buses until the railway bridge at Mills Hill was rebuilt in 1934.

Then, on 15th April 1927 Oldham launched a service to Halifax running over the route of the long withdrawn shuttle between Grains Bar and Denshaw. Jointly operated with North Western Road Car and Halifax Corporation, it ran via Greetland and Elland. Oldham gave it the route letter H, the next available letter but coincidentally also standing for Halifax. When Oldham replaced its single-deckers on the route with double-deckers, the West Riding County Council alleged that they were causing damage to the roads. So Oldham cut back the service to Denshaw, having already agreed this with North Western as part of a much bigger deal. Halifax also withdrew leaving North Western to operate the service on its own and eventually, in conjunction with the Yorkshire Woollen District Company, to expand it to run between Manchester and Bradford. John Hirst, trading as Ripponden and District Motor Services, also ran between Manchester and Halifax via Oldham and Ripponden. This service had commenced in 1925 but he gave it up to North Western and Yorkshire Woollen in 1936 to concentrate on his coaching and haulage business.

The immediate effect of the agreement with North Western was the creation of two jointly operated services. On 30th July 1927, service B was extended at both ends, from Royton through Cowlishaw and Shaw to Newhey and from Failsworth to Woodhouses. The section of route from Wren's Nest to Newhey, which but for the intervention of the First World War would have been an Oldham tram line, ran with North Western fares and conditions. The new service served to counter proposals by both Robinsons Coaches and Holt Bros to run express services between Newhey and Manchester via Royton. Then on 12th August 1927 a new service J commenced between Oldham and Greenfield via Lees, Grotton and Grasscroft.

A further seven buses were delivered during 1927, all on three-axle chassis. The first two, 28 and 29, were the WL6 model supplied by Karrier of Huddersfield with single-deck bodies built by Short Brothers of Rochester who had previously bodied the ill-fated trolleybuses. The other five were Guy's forward control FCX model, also with three axles but bodied by Roe. The first three were 39-seat single-deckers and the other two 56-seat double-deckers. They were numbered 30-34.

By the end of 1927 the following services were being operated:

A	Scouthead-Oldham-Chapel Road
B	New Hey-Royton-Woodhouses
C	Oldham-Middleton Junction
D	Oldham-Coalshaw Green
E	Oldham-Mossley
F	Shaw-Royton-Middleton
G	Oldham-Abbey Hills
H	Oldham-Halifax
J	Oldham-Greenfield.

With local demand satisfied for the time being the Tramways Committee turned their minds to greater things.

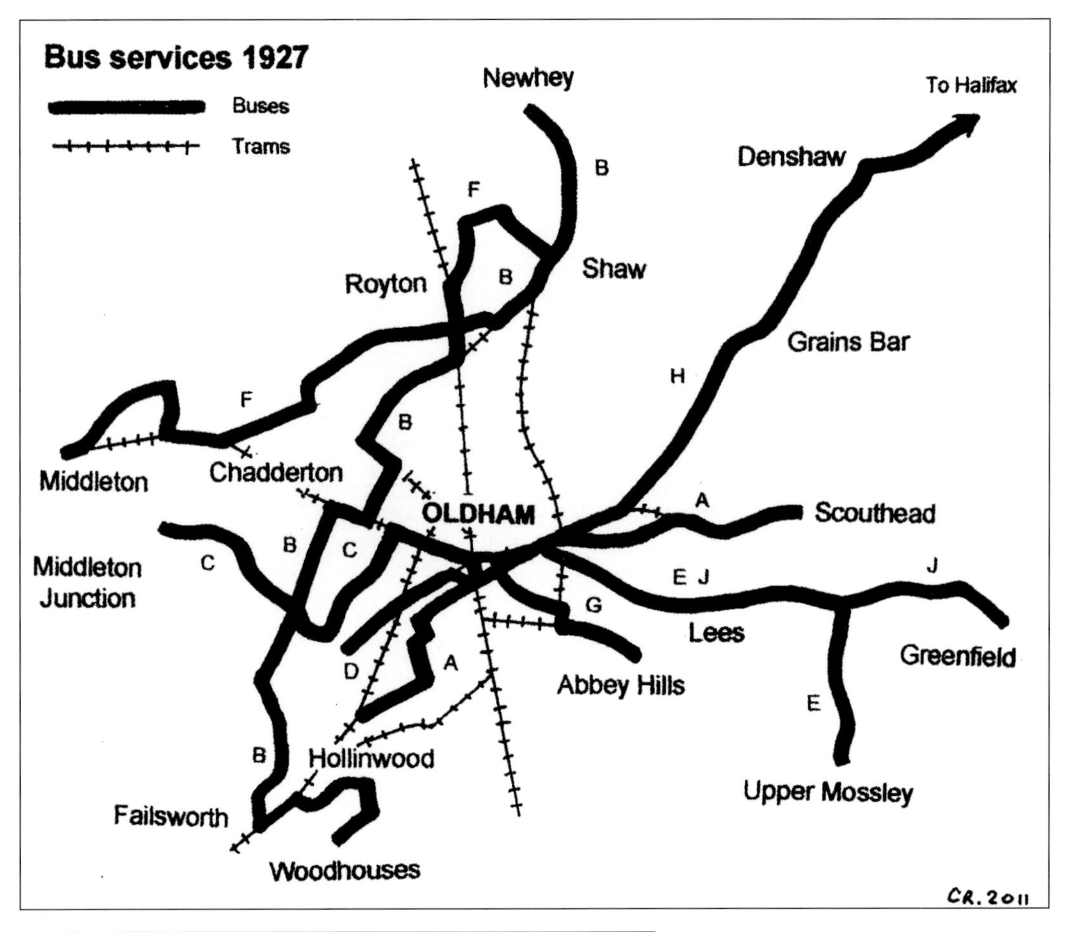

Number 20 (BU 4511) was the last of three Roe-bodied GUY BX buses delivered in 1926. The normal-control driving position with a double-deck body was an unusual combination and was unpopular with the drivers who complained of the poor nearside visibility. However, judging by Guy's publicity material on the following pages the company was very proud of its design and the bus remained in service for eight years before ending its days in comparative peace as a pavilion at the Oldham Cricket Club ground. ***(all STA)***

PIONEERS OF THE SIX-WHEELED DOUBLE DECK BUS

GUY 56-seater Six-wheeled Bus for Oldham Corporation.

Oldham Corporation have sent a repeat order for seven of these vehicles.

ALSO

FIRST to introduce One-Man Operated Single-Deck Buses with emergency door controls operated from three different parts of the vehicle.

FIRST to develop Low Loading Buses with One Step.

THE ONLY manufacturers who have for years past produced a 30-Seater which comes under the Ministry of Transport proposed weight regulations.

PIONEERS of the low loading Promenade Runa-about. Etc., etc.

LATEST FEATHERS IN OUR CAP:—

The following Corporations order Guy Six-wheeled 50/60 Passenger Vehicles:—

BIRMINGHAM OLDHAM LEEDS SHEFFIELD LIVERPOOL
MORECAMBE NORWICH SALFORD WOLVERHAMPTON READING.

Also orders for single deck, 16 to 40 seaters, from the following Corporations:—Ashton-under-Lyne, Burton-on-Trent, Blackpool, Barrow, Birkenhead, Colne, Gt. Yarmouth, Leeds, Lincoln, Liverpool, Norwich, Reading, Rio-de-Janeiro, Sheffield, Wolverhampton.

GUY MOTORS LIMITED, Wolverhampton, London & the Colonies.

When writing to Advertisers please mention this Journal

GREATER SAFETY
OF GUY SIX-WHEELED VEHICLES.

1. ELIMINATION OF WHEEL SPIN
2. SKID PROOF
3. HALVED AXLE WEIGHT
4. NO BURST TYRE DANGER
5. FOUR WHEEL BRAKES
6. LOW CENTRE OF GRAVITY
7. 75 per cent. LESS SHOCK
8. WILL GO ANYWHERE
9. GREATER TRACTIVE EFFORT
10. LESS TRACTIVE RESISTANCE

The low centre of gravity of the Guy Six-Wheeled 'Bus enables a tilting angle of over 50 deg. to be obtained; this is far in excess of anything given on four wheels. In the position shown, the vehicle was perfectly balanced and could be rocked either way over a small angle with the pressure of a finger. It will be seen that the rope is slack and was merely there as a precautionary measure.

Goods: 1 to 5 tons.
Passengers: 16 to 70 seats.

GUY MOTORS LTD., Wolverhampton and London.

The express services

By 1927 municipal tramway undertakings were coming under increasing pressure from independent bus operators creaming off revenue from their networks. Oldham had solved this problem by concluding its agreement with North Western, but neighbouring Manchester was perceived as a revenue goldmine with North Western, Ribble and a host of small independents actively trying to gain a foothold. One of these was JR Tognarelli of Bolton who had established a charabanc business after the First World War. Like many others he had run during the 1926 General Strike and had gone into regular bus operation afterwards. By the following year he was running his exotically painted lavender and silver buses between Chadderton Town Hall and Manchester via Broadway and Newton Heath. Holt Brothers, by now trading as Yelloway Motor Services, had also reappeared on the scene, running an express service between Rochdale and Manchester via Royton and Chadderton.

But now, Henry Mattinson, Manchester's forward thinking General Manager, decided to take the battle to the enemy, and proposed a network of cross-city express services within his operating area. The idea appealed to Manchester's neighbours and in August 1927 Oldham hosted a conference attended by representatives from Ashton-under-Lyne, Bolton, Bury, Manchester, Oldham, Rochdale, Salford and Stockport Corporations and the SHMD Board. Agreement was reached in principle to create a co-ordinated network of jointly-operated through services between Manchester and the various towns around, stopping only at tramway fare stages and with a higher minimum fare. Although it was originally intended to be confined to the municipal undertakings, by virtue of its existing joint operations North Western came into the scheme from an early date.

The story of the Manchester-centred network is best known, but Oldham had interests of its own and in fact the first express service in Oldham had nothing to do with Manchester. While generally it was possible to get direct to Manchester from most parts of the conurbation, travel between towns on the perimeter often involved one or more changes. During 1927 the SHMD Board had proposed an express service between Hyde and Rochdale via Ashton and Oldham but this came to nothing. Then on 17th January 1928 the Managers of the Rochdale, Oldham and Ashton-under-Lyne undertakings met and agreed proposals for a joint express service between Rochdale and Ashton via Royton, Oldham and Hathershaw. Oldham would provide two buses and Rochdale and Ashton one each in proportion to the mileage in each area. The service started on 21st February 1928 and would eventually be numbered 7 to fall in with Rochdale's new service numbering scheme.

Oldham's first involvement in the Manchester network came two weeks later on 8th March when Manchester's Gatley to Hollinwood service was extended alternately to Shaw (Wren's Nest) via Featherstall Road and Royton and to Scouthead via Manchester Road, Oldham town centre, Huddersfield Road and Waterhead, both Oldham and North Western taking a share of the operation. On 24th September 1928 a short-lived service was introduced between Manchester and Thornham Summit via Hollinwood, Featherstall Road and Royton.

Eight months later on 15th May 1929 the Manchester expresses were re-organised, the Summit service being withdrawn and the Gatley to Scouthead service extended to run from Gatley to Uppermill alternately via Scouthead and via Lees. Splitting these journeys was a circular service between Oldham and Uppermill, designated P by Oldham although North Western did not display a number. A new express bus was also introduced between Greenfield and Manchester (Lower Mosley Street) via Ashton Road, Copster Hill Road and Hollins Road and service J was withdrawn. Finally, on 12th July 1929, the two Uppermill services, both of which reversed in the middle of Uppermill, were joined to run as a circular

For some time Royton Council had been pressing for a service between Royton town centre and the Heyside area, an outlying part of Royton sandwiched between Oldham and Shaw and only served by the trams running between those two points. So eventually on 9th December alternate journeys on service B were diverted along Blackshaw Lane and Oldham Road. There would be further developments but for the present we need to go back a few years.

Buses for Trams

Most of Oldham's tramway network had been in continuous use for over 20 years, a period which included the First World War when only the minimum of maintenance had taken place. The infrastructure was quite literally wearing out and increasingly there were complaints about the rough riding of the cars and the noise and vibration on curves and pointwork. Further, road traffic was increasing and the resulting congestion in the narrow streets, compounded by long stretches of single track with passing loops was making the trams less attractive.

People tend to look back to the so-called glory days when a profitable tram service contributed income and subsidised the town's rates. However, closer inspection usually shows that the main reason for this was that insufficient allowance was made for replacement of the track and overhead at the end of its working life, often because the capital equipment was written down over a longer period than the reality. In this respect Oldham was neither better nor worse than any other undertaking at the time, none of whom had any previous experience of running heavy tramcars at high frequencies and tended to be over optimistic. But whatever the reasons by the mid-'twenties serious capital expenditure was needed and in a time of financial stringency there just wasn't enough money to carry it out

There was also another problem in that the Tramways Act had fixed leases at 21 years and those in the surrounding districts were starting to run out. The Lees lease expired on 31st July 1924 and Oldham met Lees, together with Royton and Crompton whose leases were due to end on 31st December 1925, to discuss the matter. Meanwhile the Lees lease was extended temporarily and eventually, after lengthy discussions, all three were renewed for a further 21 years. With the benefit of hindsight his seems rather short-sighted in view of the amount of reconstruction work that would be needed and the relatively low cost of the bus alternative. All three districts looked at the possibility of running the services themselves, but after working out the implications caution prevailed.

The track was still deteriorating so during 1926 Mr Jackson, who by then had succeeded Mr Chamberlain as General Manager, opened discussions with all three districts on the insertion of a clause in the lease to allow buses to be substituted for trams when it became necessary. Royton and Crompton would not agree, but after lengthy negotiations Lees did, so on 12th January 1927 the Tramways Committee, having considered and rejected the use of trolleybuses, recommended that the Lees Road tram service be abandoned and replaced by a service of motor buses. This decision was endorsed by the full Council on 26th January 1928. The Council then applied to the Ministry of Transport for loan sanction to borrow £39,790, or over two million pounds at today's prices, for 14 new buses and to lift the tram tracks and reinstate the highway. However, the Ministry's view was that while the purchase of new buses qualified for a loan, the highway works were Oldham's responsibility and reduced the amount accordingly.

The last tram ran to Lees on 1st May 1928, buses on service O taking over the following day and running beyond County End through Springhead to Grotton with trams continuing to work between the Market Place and Hollinwood. It was not long before a complaint was received from the LMS Railway that the heavy double-decker buses now working the route were causing damage to the bridge over the Oldham to Greenfield line at Springhead station and suggesting that either the service be diverted or that Oldham Corporation pay for the bridge to be strengthened. Oldham were not prepared to consider either option and legal action was threatened, but it seems to have been largely bluff as nothing more was heard. The problem disappeared in the late sixties when the cutting was filled in after the line was closed.

The day after the buses were introduced, the Tramways Committee inspected the Ripponden Road line as far as Moorside and concluded that it was in a very unsatisfactory condition. It was decided to abandon the route and buses took over between the Market Place and Grains Bar on Christmas Eve 1928, a somewhat strange time to introduce such an important service revision. This time the buses carried the service numbers of the trams they replaced; 5 for Grains Bar and 6 for Moorside. The tram tracks were retained as far as Watersheddings for special services for Oldham Rugby League club's matches and trams continued to run between the Market Place and Hollinwood. via Hollins Road.

To work the new services and the other routes which were introduced during the year, 22 new buses were acquired during 1928. These were to be a mixture of Karrier and Guy 3-axle chassis, carrying both single-deck and double-deck bodies from various makers. Number 35 was a Karrier DD6/1 with a double-deck body by Hall, Lewis, later to become Park Royal Coachworks, which seated 70 passengers, a huge number for those days. It had been exhibited at the 1927 Commercial Motor Show and consequently arrived after number 36, a Guy FCX with bodywork by Short Brothers with an even greater seating capacity of 72! The arrival of these extremely large buses provoked a swift reaction from the Ministry of Transport, which initially refused to sanction their use as their unladen weight was above that permitted by the regulations. Two seats were removed to bring down the weight and allow them to run, but the next double-deckers would only seat 66.

Numbers 37-42 were six Karrier CL6s with more conventional 33-seat single-deck bodies for the express services. They were followed by six Karrier DD6s 43-48 and eight Guy FCXs 49-56, all with identical 66-seat double-deck bodies from English Electric of Preston who had supplied all of Oldham's trams. All the six-wheel vehicles were notoriously thirsty and often had to be topped up with petrol during their duties, usually in the Market Place until the police intervened. Unpopular as they may have been at Oldham, the last eight Guys lasted until 1936 when they migrated *en bloc* to the flat coastal areas of southern Essex, running for Canvey and District Motor Services for a further two years.

More conventional than the three double-deckers was number 22 (BU 5475), a basically similar BKX chassis but fitted with a single-deck body. Delivered in 1927, 22 was one of those taken by Leyland in 1934 in part exchange for new buses. ***(STA)***

Number 30 (BU 4840) was a forward-control Guy FCX with a 39-seat Roe body delivered in 1927. It lasted for eight years and later became a caravan at Moorside. ***(STA)***

Guy's FCX chassis was also available as a double-decker, Oldham acquiring two examples in 1927. Number 33 (BU 4843) is pictured above being washed in the Henshaw Street depot. ***(MMT)***

Oldham's largest bus until the Leyland PD3s of 1964, number 36 (BU 5173), the 72-seat Short Bros-bodied Guy FCX of 1928, is shown being fuelled as it comes into depot after duty. These pictures are two of a series taken by the Corporation's official photographer in the Henshaw Street depot during 1928. ***(MMT)***

More changes

During 1929 JR Tognarelli, the Bolton-based independent operator, had been running a service between Chadderton Town Hall and Manchester. Tognarelli had applied several times for licences in the Manchester area, but had been unsuccessful on each occasion. Nevertheless, he had carried on running illegally, but now ill health and pressure from the authorities caused him to pull out and sell his business to Bolton, Manchester, Oldham and Salford Corporations and Lancashire United Transport. Oldham's share of the purchase was his Chadderton service which they took over on 9th December 1929. With the route Oldham acquired two Associated Daimler buses, WH 1352 with a Bell 32-seat body dating from 1928 which they numbered 57 and WH 1441 with a Burlingham 32-seat body which was less than a year old and received the number 58.

For a short time the route remained unchanged while Oldham considered what to do with it. Then on 19th May 1930 it was integrated into a new service 2 running from Newhey to Manchester (Lower Mosley Street) via Shaw, Royton, Chadderton and Broadway, jointly operated with Manchester Corporation and North Western. At the same time service B was diverted from the Sportsman's Arms on Broadway along Foxdenton Lane to Middleton Junction and then via Mills Hill Road and Oldham Road to Middleton. It was initially operated by Oldham who seemed anxious to get rid of it and on 29th November 1930 it was taken over by North Western, eventually becoming their service 159.

Four weeks later on 16th May another express service was introduced between Oldham and Northenden via Werneth, joint with Manchester and numbered 34.

For some time there had been calls for the redevelopment of the Market Place and plans were drawn up which included the provision of an 'omnibus centre' or bus station on the north side of High Street in the area known as 'The Green'. It was decided to promote a bill in Parliament and the work was costed at £90,000, a huge sum in those days. Discussions dragged on but in the end, in a time of economic depression, it simply could not be afforded and the proposal was finally abandoned early in 1931. Oldham would have to do without its bus station until PTE days.

As the 'twenties passed into the 'thirties momentous events, both international and domestic, would combine to change the shape of the passenger transport industry.

OLDHAM CORPORATION TRAMWAYS.

DENSHAW & MOSSLEY

MOTOR OMNIBUS ROUTES.

On and after SATURDAY NEXT, JULY 20th, 1929,

The Following **FARES** and **STAGES** will come into Operation.

Oldham & Denshaw Route.

Oldham G.P.O.
1d. Mumps Bridge
1d. 1d. Asa Lees
2d. 1d. 1d. Black Horse
2d. 2d. 1d. 1d. Pumping Station
3d. 2d. 2d. 1d. 1d. Moorside
3d. 3d. 2d. 2d. 1d. 1d. Waggon and Horses
4d. 3d. 3d. 2d. 2d. 1d. 1d. Grains Bar
5d. 4d. 4d. 3d. 3d. 2d. 2d. 1d. Bankside Cottages
5d. 5d. 4d. 3d. 3d. 2d. 2d. 1d. 1d. Golden Fleece
6d 5d. 5d. 4d. 4d. 3d. 3d. 2d. 2d. 1d. Denshaw

Return Fare.

OLDHAM G.P.O. and DENSHAW ... ... 9d.

Special Workman's Fares.

G.P.O. CLEGG STREET and DENSHAW ... ... 6d. RETURN
ASA LEES' WORKS and DENSHAW ... ... 5d. RETURN

Oldham Town Hall & Mossley

Oldham Town Hall
... Mumps Bridge
1d. ... Balfour Street
2d. 1d. 1d. Gibraltar Street
2d. 2d. 1d. 1d. Lees, County End
3d. 3d. 2d. 2d. 1d. Grotton, Station Road
4d. 4d. 3d. 3d. 2d. 1d. Lane
5d. 5d. 4d. 4d. 3d. 2d. 1d. Mossley Boundary
6d. 6d. 5d. 5d. 4d. 3d. 2d. 1d. Mossley, Brookbottom

Return Fares.

OLDHAM TOWN HALL and LANE ... ... 6d.
LEES COUNTY END and MOSSLEY BROOKBOTTOM... ... ... 6d.
OLDHAM TOWN HALL and MOSSLEY BROOKBOTTOM ... ... 10d.
OLDHAM TOWN HALL and MOSSLEY BROOKBOTTOM ... WEEKLY TICKET 4s.

C. JACKSON,
General Manager & Engineer.

General Manager's Office,
Wallshaw Depot, Oldham.
16th, July, 1929.

J. ALLAN HANSON & SON, LTD., CROFTBANK WORKS, CROSS STREET, OLDHAM

Opposite page. Number 54 (BU 5561) was one of the final batch of Guy FCXs with the slightly smaller English Electric 66-seat body specified to keep the weight within Ministry of Transport regulations. These eight buses were already obsolete when they were delivered in 1928 but lasted for eight years before passing to Canvey and District Motor Services in Essex. ***(STA)***

5 – *THE TURBULENT THIRTIES*

A great step forward

The 1930s, with its trade depression, mass unemployment and political unrest culminating in the Second World War, were what the old Chinese philosopher would have called 'interesting times'. But they were also genuinely interesting for the great changes in all aspects of the transport industry that happened during the decade.

So far, although they had grown in size and power over the years, buses still showed their tramway origins. With its high chassis and basically single-deck body and a totally unrelated box-like upper deck mounted on top, a double-deck bus looked like nothing more than a petrol-engined tramcar without rails. But by the end of the previous decade bus design had taken a great step forward. At the end of 1927 Leyland introduced its Tiger single-decker and Titan double-decker, followed in 1929 by AEC's similar Regal and Regent, and all other manufacturers quickly followed suit. What these and all subsequent designs had in common was a drop-frame chassis which allowed a much lower floor and, in the case of the double-deckers, a well proportioned body which was designed as a whole rather than the top deck looking as if it had been put on as an afterthought. These new buses offered standards of comfort far superior to existing designs – and most contemporary trams.

Oldham's first buses of the new era were four Roe-bodied Leyland Tiger TS3 single-deckers which arrived in 1931, numbered 59-62. Painted in the same crimson lake and white livery as used on the trams, they looked very smart and modern. They were followed the following year by five more single-deckers and eight double-deckers. The single-deckers 63-7 were the longer TS4 model, the first four bodied by Roe and the fifth by local builder Shearing and Crabtree. The double-deckers, numbered 68-75, were Leyland Titan TD2s with Leyland 51-seat bodies to the new 6-bay piano-front design which was popular at the time. More than anything else the modern lines of these eight buses epitomised the huge leap forward in design from the Guys and Karriers, some of which were still only four years old. The new Leylands were to be the last petrol-engined buses purchased as the next major development was just around the corner.

Reference has already been made to the excessive thirst of the big petrol-engined six-wheel double-deckers. The fuel bill has always been a major concern of transport operators and Oldham was no different. By the end of the twenties the compression ignition engine running

The first buses of the new era were four Leyland Tiger TS3s with Roe bodies delivered in 1931. Number 61 (BU 6762) poses outside the factory showing service number 14 on the front but carrying route branding for the Newhey to Manchester service. ***(STA)***

Above. Five more Leyland Tigers came in 1932, four bodied by Roe and a fifth one by the local firm of Shearing and Crabtree. One of the Roe-bodied examples poses for an official photograph in the depot. These buses would run in Oldham for sixteen years before passing to other operators for further service. ***(MMT)***

Below. Number 68 (BU 7107) was the first of eight Leyland Titan TD2 models with Leyland 51-seat bodies, the classic design which revolutionised the industry in the early thirties. It is pictured at Mumps picking up passengers for Lees when new. ***(MMT)***

on heavy oil was becoming widely used in industry and shipping and it was thought that with further development to fit it into road vehicles it would be a cheaper and more reliable alternative. So, in December 1930 members of the Tramways Committee visited Sheffield to look at a couple of examples of oil-engined buses running in the city. However, while recognising the potential, the committee deferred any further action.

Neighbouring Manchester had purchased a former Crossley oil-engined demonstrator early in 1931 and at the same time Rochdale Corporation had experimented with a diesel engine in one of a batch of new Crossleys then being delivered. Both operators were so impressed that they quickly adopted the new technology as standard. However, Oldham was more cautious and it was late in 1932 before a Leyland demonstrator was tried. There was then an attempt to use creosote oil in one of the Guys but it failed miserably, only lasting for ten days before being abandoned. Following this a Leyland diesel engine was fitted to Titan number 72 early in 1933. Finally convinced by the success of this experiment diesel engines were specified for future deliveries.

The first of these was a batch of eight further Leyland Titan TD2 double-deckers which arrived in July 1933, this time with English Electric 52-seat bodies. They became 10-17, taking the numbers of the 1925 AEC 507s that had now been withdrawn. They were followed a month later by 21-29, nine Leyland Tiger TS4s with 32-seat front-entrance single-deck bodies by Roe, replacing an equivalent number of Guy and Karrier single-deckers.

The 1930 Road Traffic Act

The growth of bus services in the late 1920s was beginning to put a strain on the existing regulatory system initially authorised by the Town Police Clauses Acts of 1847 and 1849 and designed to deal with hackney carriages, whereby prospective operators had to obtain licences from each individual local authority along the line of the proposed route. This did not matter much so long as the bus routes were only short feeders to the trams, but as services became longer and began to cross municipal boundaries it started to cause problems. A prime example was Oldham's Uppermill to Gatley service which needed separate licences from Cheadle and Gatley, Manchester, Failsworth, Oldham and Saddleworth Councils, which then had to be endorsed by the Lancashire, Cheshire and West Riding of Yorkshire County Councils. Not only that, but buses also had to be licenced similarly and were required to carry a hackney carriage plate for each of the areas in which they operated. Little wonder then that some of the smaller independents opted to run illegally for as long as they could get away with it.

The main purpose of Herbert Morrison's Road Traffic Act was to streamline the licensing procedure by taking it away from the multitude of local authorities, each with its own independent transport policy, and concentrating it into a number of Traffic Areas presided over by Government appointed Traffic Commissioners. The intention was to simplify the process and bring consistency to the decision-making. So far as the passenger industry was concerned it covered the issue and renewal of Road Service Licences, Public Service Vehicle Licences and Driver and Conductor Licences. Trams and trolleybuses were not covered by the regulations. Oldham came within Area C, the new North Western Traffic Area with its headquarters at Sunlight House in Manchester. The Chairman of the Commissioners was Mr (later Sir) William Chamberlain who had been Oldham's General Manager from May 1918 until April 1925 and who resigned from his position as General Manager of the Belfast Corporation Tramways to take up the post.

All existing operators now had to apply for licences to continue the services they were already running. However, transitional regulations were issued on 9th February 1931 under which all vehicles and services operating on that date were allowed to continue running subject to any conditions then in force, until such time as the applications for new licences could be heard and determined. The Minister of Transport made it clear, however, that permission to continue an existing service did not carry with it any rights, and the Traffic Commissioners would not be placed under any obligation when they came to consider the grant of the substantive licence for these services.

Established bodies, such as local authorities, other operators and the railway companies, were able to object to applications, even if the services had been running for a considerable time, although they would have to put up convincing arguments

Above
Number 21 (BU 7608), the first of a batch of nine Roe-bodied Leyland TS4s, was delivered in 1933. It ran in Oldham until 1928 and was then sold to Leeds City Transport for further service. ***(STA)***

Right
Before ordering buses for future tramway conversions a Crossley Mancunian (upper) and a Leyland Titan TD3, both with oil engines, were bought during 1934 for evaluation. The Crossley, number 57 (BU 7945), remained in the fleet until 1950 when it was sold to a showman, while the Leyland was withdrawn two years earlier, passing to Dimbleby of Ashover, Derbyshire. The tests came out in favour of the Leyland which became the dominant maker of Oldham buses until the end. ***(STA)***

in support of their objections. Generally, town services operated by the local councils continued unchallenged. The majority of objections were against the longer distance inter-town services, particularly the expresses, where the railway companies seized the opportunity to reopen old arguments and get a second bite at the cherry. In addition there was growing concern over traffic congestion, particularly in Manchester city centre, which the railways and the taxi operators exploited in a bid to get the express services withdrawn.

Oldham was by now involved in six express services, five of which were part of the Manchester network. Three of these, 10 (Greenfield to Lower Mosley Street) and 13/14 (Uppermill to Gatley), were split in Manchester city centre and cut back to Parker Street bus station from 25th October 1931, 34 (Oldham to Northenden) following two weeks later. Service 2 (Newhey to Lower Mosley Street) escaped the net for the time being, perhaps because it was integrated with Manchester's 2A (New Moston to Firswood) which remained a cross-city service until it faded away in SELNEC days. All five routes were further cut back to Stevenson Square as a wartime economy on 28th December 1942. The sixth service was 7 (Rochdale-Oldham-Ashton) which survived objections from the railway companies and continued operating unchanged for a number of years.

The SELNEC Scheme

Within the Manchester area there had long been a high degree of co-ordination and joint working of services between the various operators, both municipal and company, dating back to the early tramway days. After the demise of the abortive joint committee comprising municipal undertakings either side of the Pennines, Oldham had become involved in the great express network and by this time was running a number of services jointly with three other municipal operators as well as the North Western Road Car Company.

Following the implementation of the 1930 Road Traffic Act, discussions took place on the subject of a Joint Municipal Passenger Transport Board for South East Lancashire and East Cheshire, known as SELNEC, the brainchild of Manchester's General Manager, R Stuart Pilcher. In 1931 representatives of Ashton, Bolton, Bury, Leigh, Manchester, Oldham, Rochdale, Salford, SHMD, Stockport and Wigan met to discuss broad principles of a merger. Leigh and Wigan soon withdrew as they had little common interest with the rest of the group, but Manchester continued to host a series of conferences on the subject.

There were, however, two main stumbling blocks to agreement; fears of the loss of local influence over services and fares, and worries about how the different outstanding capital debts would be treated. One by one operators withdrew and by 1935 only Manchester, Oldham, Rochdale and Salford were still interested. Rochdale withdrew from the scheme in the April and a meeting of the three remaining operators took place on 17th July 1935 when it was decided not to promote the necessary Bill.

Nothing more came of the idea, although a series of conferences of all the municipal operators in the area, plus Ribble, North Western and Lancashire United and the LMS and LNE Railways, took place the following year which again came to nothing and it was not for another 32 years that the 1968 Transport Act would create the Passenger Transport Authorities and Oldham Corporation Transport would be no more.

Consolidation

The first few years of the decade were a period of consolidation. With most areas away from the tram routes now served by buses there were no major changes to the network and activity was confined to serving small pockets of new housing. For some time there had been pressure for a service to the growing council estates at Albert Mount and Derker lying between Shaw Road and Huddersfield Road. Plans were drawn up for a service utilising the long abandoned tram route along Egerton Street and then entering the estate via Shaw Road and Derker Street. However, not for the first time, the idea of using Egerton Street was abandoned and the proposal was dropped. But the problem would not go away and after several more requests and refusals Derker finally got its buses. On 30th April 1932 a service started running along Huddersfield Road and Barry Street, extending across town along the Chadderton Road tram route to the junction of Burnley Lane and Broadway, taking the now vacant letter B. Then on 4th September express services 13 and 14 were co-ordinated with service 10 and rerouted via Ashton Road, Copster Hill Road and Hollins Road. It must have been frustrating for the residents of the Oldham Edge area having to walk into town while buses were passing them running light to and from depot and from time to time requests were made for a bus service. But it was another two years before, on 24th March 1934, the short route R commenced between the Star Inn and the Royton boundary at Booth Hill Road via King Street, the Market Place, Henshaw Street and Godson Street. Then on 6th January 1935 service B was extended across Broadway to new housing further along Burnley Lane. The service turned back by reversing into Birch Avenue, the terminus however, being better known to the locals by the more picturesque name of Clogger Hill.

Royton Council pressed for a local circular service around Rochdale Road, Sheepfoot Lane, Westhulme Avenue, Chadderton Road and Featherstall Road. The Committee discussed it, deferred it and finally forgot it. Now, nearly 80 years later the area is served by a local circular route.

Hard times

The economic situation was beginning to bite, with rising costs and declining revenue due to the number of people unemployed having an adverse effect on the Department's finances. Economies were made and some services were reduced, the former tram routes running at higher frequencies coming under particular scrutiny. On 20th October 1930 alternate journeys on the Grotton service (O) had been cut back to Lees (County End), although this was as much to do with the provision of suitable turning facilities as saving mileage.

Ripponden Road services 5 (Grains Bar) and 6 (Moorside) terminated at the Market Place while the Denshaw service (H) turned at the Town Hall and ran via Union Street. It was decided to co-ordinate the services on a reduced frequency, all turning at the Town Hall, but this proved unpopular and the original pattern was quickly reinstated with services 5 and 6 running to the Market Place via Union Street and George Street and returning along High Street and Yorkshire Street. With spare cars available, consideration was also given to reinstating the tram service as far as Moorside with an express bus to Denshaw. However, the track in Ripponden Road which had been unused for over two years would have been too expensive to return to operational condition so the track was lifted during 1933 and the road reinstated using unemployed labour under the Relief of Unemployment scheme.

With mass unemployment there was a growing lobby for the use of home produced electricity for traction instead of imported oil. Since the 1925 fiasco technology had improved dramatically and the Committee looked at replacing the buses on the Lees Road and Ripponden Road routes by trolleybuses but in the end decided against it.

A fares increase was considered, but was thought to be too politically sensitive at a time when everyone was having to cut their spending to make ends meet. However, in an effort to boost ridership, weekend and off-peak return fares at one and a half times the price of a single journey at a minimum fare of three halfpence on Saturdays and Sundays were introduced for a six month trial period in August 1931. However, this was not successful, and the scheme was withdrawn at the end of the trial.

Economies were made in the workshops and staffing levels reduced, but after protests from the Trade Unions and a threat of strike action most of the dismissed men were reinstated.

Tramway abandonment

Although the Lees Road and Ripponden Road routes had been replaced by buses in 1928, there was at this time no overall policy to abandon trams, each route being looked at on an individual basis. However, the infrastructure was now over 30 years old and was getting to the stage where it was wearing out and it was uneconomical to reconstruct it.

With tramway replacement in mind a Leyland demonstrator fitted with a torque converter was tried out late in 1933. The torque converter provided a fully automatic transmission apart from a manually engaged direct drive which was the equivalent of the top gear. It was controlled by a selector lever replacing the normal gear lever, with four positions, converter, direct, neutral and reverse. The torque converter did away with the need for the driver to change gear and some operators took large numbers of these vehicles for tramway conversions, considering it easier to train tram drivers on them rather than on buses with a

Three Leyland Tiger TS6 single-deckers with Roe full-fronted bodywork entered the fleet in 1934 for use on the express services. In the photograph number 20 (BU 8256) is pictured outside the Roe works, showing the route branding on red glass above the upper saloon windows. The interior view below shows the comfortable seating, luggage racks and saloon heater, setting standards which would not be out of place on long distance routes at that time. ***(both STA)***

conventional clutch and crash gearbox. Oldham, as ever, was more concerned with the downsides of lower power and higher fuel consumption and showed no further interest.

In May 1934 the newly renamed Transport Committee agreed to Mr Richards' proposals to abandon the Chadderton Road, Middleton Road and Shaw Road routes and substitute buses. This caused problems as the leases on the tracks in Crompton and Royton had been renewed in 1925 and were not due to expire until 31st December 1946. Negotiations on the amount of compensation Oldham would have to pay on the outstanding period of the leases, plus the cost of reinstating the highway, were lengthy, but agreement was eventually reached on sums of £2,000 to Crompton and £3,200 to Royton, both Districts undertaking to co-operate with Oldham on the continuing operation of bus services in their areas.

Meanwhile, in advance of placing what would be a large order for buses for the coming conversions, a Crossley Mancunian with a Crossley VR6 oil engine and Roe 53-seat body and a Leyland Titan TD3 with English Electric 52-seat body were purchased for evaluation. They were numbered 57 and 58 respectively, 58 having a deeper radiator than the TD2s, experience having shown that this was needed to provide more cooling for the diesel engine. Tests showed that while the Crossley was marginally more powerful, which would be an advantage on the hilly Oldham routes, the Leyland was more economical and reliable. The latter qualities prevailed and, with the exception of a small batch of five Crossleys the following year and six Daimlers in 1937, all subsequent Oldham buses were Leylands until after the Second World War.

Three Leyland Tiger TS6 single-deckers, 18-20, arrived in 1934. They carried full-fronted Roe bodies and were route-branded for the express services, Uppermill, Newhey and Greenfield respectively. Six more Leyland Titan TD3s with Roe 54-seat bodies, 30-35, came soon after and replaced more of the older straight-framed buses, leaving only 14 buses in the fleet, all Guy FCXs, more than five years old.

With the exception of the now defunct bus station, plans were well advanced for the redevelopment of the Market Place. The Borough Engineer also wanted to remodel the junction of West Street and Rochdale Road, so it was decided to simplify the track layout through the town centre and abandon the tram services coming in from the north side.

In this impressive official photograph, numbers 76 to 101, all the Roe-bodied Leyland TD3s in the big 1935 delivery, are lined up in numerical order in the Wallshaw Street depot before entering service. ***(MMT)***

Number 91 (BU 8441) was one of the 26 Roe-bodied Leyland TD3s delivered in 1935 for conversion of the Shaw and Middleton Road tram routes pictured on the previous page. It was withdrawn in 1948 and passed to a showman. The photographs on the left show upper and lower deck interiors. Plain and functional they were typical of the period. ***(all STA)***

On 11th June 1935 the last journeys ran on tram services 3 (Market Place-Middleton) and 9 (Shaw-Market Place-Chadderton Road), buses taking over the following day. At the same time the opportunity was taken to improve links across the town centre, the replacement bus routes being

3	Shaw-Oldham-Middleton
5	Burnley Lane-Oldham-Grains Bar
6	Burnley Lane-Oldham-Moorside
59	Shaw-Oldham-Middleton-Manchester

Service 59 was an extension of Manchester Corporation's former tram route from Cannon Street to Mills Hill which followed a circuitous route via Cheetham Hill, Heaton Park and Middleton and became for many years the longest bus route operated by either undertaking, still running basically in the same form to this day. On the same day service B (Derker-Market Place-Burnley Lane) came off the Chadderton Road section and was instead diverted to Booth Hill, service R being withdrawn.

To operate the new services a total of 31 buses comprising 5 Crossley Mancunians and 26 Leyland Titan TD3s were ordered, all with Roe bodies. Crossley had shorter delivery times than Leyland and the five buses on order, numbered 1-5, arrived in December 1934 and were stored until they were needed for the conversions. The Leylands 76-101 were all delivered in the early part of 1935, most also being stored until needed. Service D was extended again in Chadderton from Coalshaw Green along Turf Lane to a new terminus at the junction of Long Lane.

While this was happening the Borough Engineer outlined plans to improve the junction of Manchester Road and Hollins Road at Hollinwood which once again would mean that the tram lines would have to be realigned. The Transport Committee considered the condition of the track in Hollins Road and Copster Hill Road and decided to abandon the route as soon as possible and ordered a further 12 buses for the conversion.

However, in an attempt to increase ridership, fares had been reduced earlier in the year. The response had been greater than anticipated so it was decided to increase the order by a further six vehicles, meanwhile borrowing two Crossley double-deckers from the manufacturers. The 18 new buses were all Leyland Titans of the latest TD4 model with a mixture of bodies. Numbers 102-4 carried metal-framed six-bay bodies by Leyland and 105 had a metal-framed 5-bay body by Metro-Cammell whilst 106-109 were bodied by English Electric and 110-119 by Roe, 116 having an experimental metal-framed body.

Once these buses arrived it was possible to convert the Hollins Road service, the last trams running on 21st December 1935, buses on service O between Grotton and the Market Place being extended to Hollinwood the following day. In all, during 1935, 44 buses had replaced 40 trams and the six remaining Guy single-deckers.

On 10th April 1936 a new service was introduced between the Town Hall and Stalybridge via Abbey Hills Road, Lees Road and Hurst Cross, skirting Ashton to the east. Although this was only an hourly service and needed just one bus except on Sundays, it was jointly worked by three different operators, Oldham and Ashton Corporations and the SHMD Board, who regularly rotated the duties between them to keep the mileage to the agreed proportions. Ashton and SHMD numbered it 8, but Oldham already had a number 8 tram so instead gave it the previously unused letter N!

Like Oldham, neighbouring Manchester had been steadily converting its tramway system to diesel buses although there was a growing faction advocating the use of trolleybuses and eventually Manchester deposited a Bill in Parliament seeking the necessary powers to run them. This would not have concerned Oldham but for two clauses in the Bill, to run trolleybuses on any public road in or outside the city and to generate the necessary electricity. Whether it was intended or not, this would have allowed Manchester to run trolleybuses anywhere in Oldham. So Oldham, along with other concerned local authorities, objected to the offending clauses and they were withdrawn.

To replace the last remaining Guy six-wheel double-deckers and to cater for the still-growing demand, a total of 12 more Leyland Titan TD4s was ordered, 36-41 bodied by English Electric and 42-47 by Roe. The influx of new buses since 1931, mainly for tramway conversions, meant that there would now be no buses in the fleet more than five years old. Then, later in the year, still concerned by the continuing increase in traffic and considering the matter too urgent

Upper. Although delivered a year later than 91, English Electric's rather antiquated 6-bay body makes Leyland TD4 number 108 (BU 8863) look the older of the pair. It was also withdrawn in 1948 but went for scrap. ***(STA)***

Centre. By comparison number 116 (BU 8974) looks far more modern with its experimental Roe 5-bay metal-framed body. It lasted longer than most of its contemporaries, being withdrawn in 1950 and passing to a showman. ***(STA)***

Lower. Another picture of an English Electric-bodied Leyland TD4, this time number 122 (BU 9623) of the 1936 batch. ***(STA)***

Roe-bodied Leyland TD4 130 (BU 9631) of the 1937 batch poses near the Roe works before delivery to Oldham. ***(STA)***

Number 178 (ABU 863), a Leyland-bodied Leyland TD5 delivered in 1938. ***(STA)***

to go through the lengthy process of external advertising, the Committee decided to place a repeat order for 12 buses without going out to tender although this was against the Council's Standing Orders. But this irregularity would cause complications, the Ministry of Transport refusing to sanction a Government loan, and the buses had to be purchased out of revenue. The buses, which arrived by the end of the year, were numbered 120-31, all Leyland Titan TD4s, again half bodied by English Electric and half by Roe.

The next tramway abandonment came the following year. On 6th November 1937 the last tram ran on the Glodwick Circular route 4 and the following day buses took over showing 4 in one direction and V the other! At the same time the original steam line between Hathershaw and Thornham Summit which had been converted to buses once before and later reinstated was finally abandoned, tram 7 being replaced by bus 9 between Hathershaw and Rochdale, jointly operated with Rochdale Corporation, and bus M on short workings in the Oldham area between Hathershaw and Summit.

These conversions needed a total of 42 buses, the first 36 being Leyland Titan TD5s 132-52 with bodies by English Electric and 153-67 bodied by Roe. The Roe bodies were to an improved design incorporating a new type of staircase which featured two half landings and, as a result, moved the bottom step further away from the platform edge making it less likely for a passenger slipping on the stairs to fall off the bus.

The remaining buses were a new departure for Oldham. Numbers 168-73 were six Roe bodied Daimler COG6s with Gardner 6LW engines built at Patricroft with transmission through a fluid flywheel and preselector gearbox. The selector pedal was heavy and if not fully depressed was liable to kick back painfully, leaving the bus free-wheeling in neutral until the pedal could be pressed back into place; not a very good situation on Oldham's hills. Although the Gardner engine was popular with many operators due to its reliability and fuel economy, it never found favour with Oldham. No more Gardner engines were bought and when 25 similar Daimlers were purchased after the war they were fitted with Daimler's own engine.

The Ministry of Transport, not too happy with Oldham over the previous tendering irregularities, summoned the Chairman and General Manager to London to explain why the lowest tender for the bodies of the last six buses had not been accepted, and would only sanction a loan for the amount of that tender, leaving Oldham with a shortfall of £2,967 which again had to come out of revenue. Only six new buses arrived during 1938, a small batch of Leyland Titan TD5s numbered 174-179, this time with Leyland's standard metal framed body.

During 1936 it had been decided to centralise the operations on the Wallshaw Street site. Accordingly, 19,000 square yards of derelict industrial land were purchased behind the tram shed and plans were drawn up for a new central garage and offices at an estimated cost of £102,000. With the new building the floor area was increased to 136,500 square feet which at that time would accommodate up to 300 buses, although as buses became longer this would come down to some 225 thirty years later. The Henshaw Street premises closed its doors on 25th May and the Hollinwood depot and workshops were sold to Ferranti Ltd

The gathering storm

It had previously been decided to replace all the trams by the end of 1939, so early in the year another 47 Roe-bodied Leyland TD5s were ordered to convert tram services 1/20 (Waterhead-Oldham-Hollinwood-Manchester) and 8 (Shaw-Royton-Hollinwood) to bus operation. Although again these were not the lowest tender there was no comment this time from the Ministry of Transport.

On 18th February 1939 Ashton-under-Lyne Corporation, although committed to trolleybus operation with modern vehicles on their joint routes with Manchester, withdrew their pioneering service between Ashton and Hathershaw. At the same time the express service 7 between Rochdale, Oldham and Ashton was withdrawn and the following day service 9 (Rochdale-Oldham-Hathershaw) was extended to Ashton providing a local service every 10 minutes between the towns. Service number 7 was then used for variations of services 3 and 59 between Chadderton Town Hall and Higginshaw.

The LMS Railway wrote giving notice of its intention to impose a 5-ton limit on the Glodwick Road bridge but Oldham continued running and although a notice was still displayed on the bridge as late as 1967, four years after the last train stopped running, buses have crossed it with no apparent problems ever since.

As 1939 rolled on the political situation in Europe worsened. The Civil Defence Act came into force and preparations were made for the inevitable outbreak of war in Europe. Civilians were enrolled in the new Local Defence Volunteers later to be renamed the Home Guard, training took place in air raid precautions and shelters were constructed in the Wallshaw Street premises. On 3rd September 1939 Britain declared war on Germany and a few days later the first of the new buses for the final tram conversions arrived.

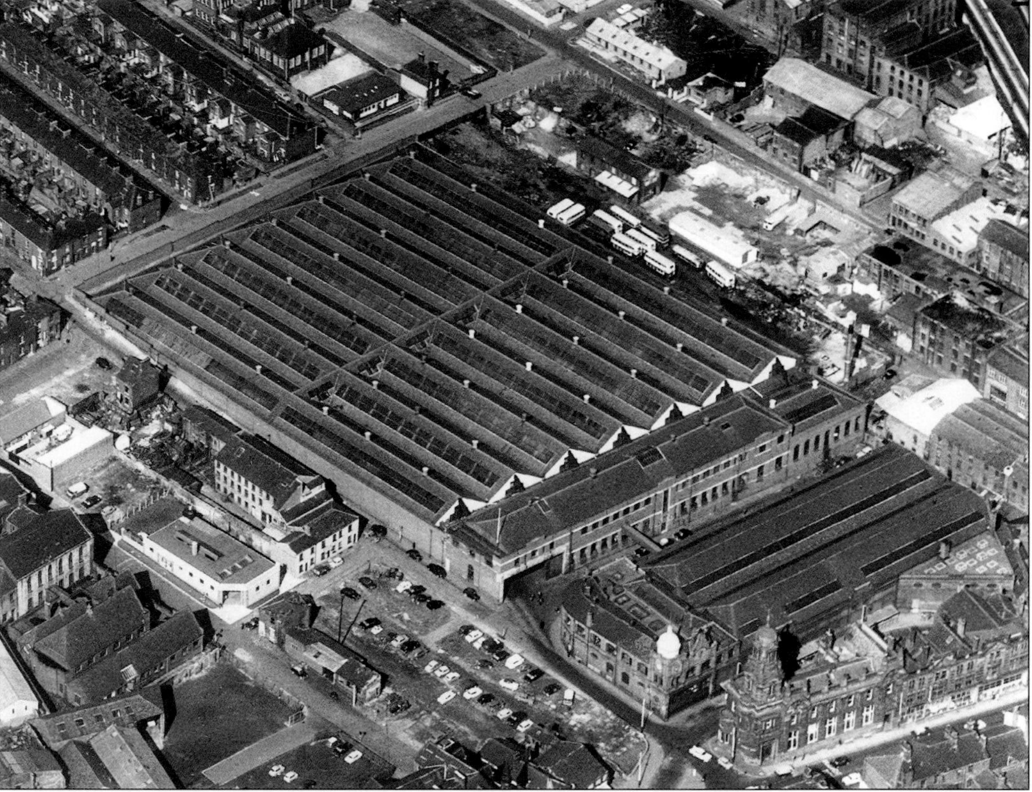

Wallshaw Street depot under construction (above) and an areal view of the complex below. ***(both STA)***

6 – *THE SECOND WORLD WAR*

Oldham at War

In Oldham the news broke as people returned from their annual Wakes holidays. Many preparations had already been made in anticipation, but now that hostilities had commenced, things started to happen quickly. A blackout was imposed with all street lights switched off, white bands were painted around lamp standards and other obstructions and white lines were also painted on kerbs at junctions and along the middle of the roads to aid visibility. Destination signs on bus stops and shelters were either painted out or removed to confuse the enemy in case of an invasion.

On the buses the offside headlamp and the destination indicators were removed and the interior saloon lighting was reduced. The front mudguards and rear corners were painted white and the white roofs in matt grey to make them less conspicuous from the air. While much of this may seem a waste of effort, it should be remembered that at the time bombing raids relied on a map, a watch, a compass and the aircrew's eyesight.

Driving conditions were hazardous, especially during the long winter nights, and it was little wonder that there were a number of fatalities, mostly involving pedestrians, even though the maximum speed limit was reduced from 30mph to 20mph during the hours of darkness. A government circular recommended that intending passengers should stand on the pavement and wave a white handkerchief or newspaper to attract the driver's attention. However, they should not risk dazzling the driver by flashing a torch at the oncoming bus unless it was masked by a handkerchief. Passengers were urged to have the correct money and to count out the coins into the conductor's hand!

Owing to the reluctance of people to travel in

One of the last pre war order, Roe-bodied Leyland TD5 number 205 (CBU 205) was eventually delivered to Oldham in 1940, a year after the outbreak of the Second World War. It is pictured on a works journey shortly before its withdrawal in 1958. ***(STA)***

the blackout there was a serious drop in revenue, but as the evenings grew lighter the buses became more crowded and revenue started to recover. Unfortunately' the price of materials, wages and fuel was also rising rapidly' resulting in increased operating costs.

With the outbreak of war regulation of transport came under the newly created Ministry of War Transport and was administered by the former Chairmen of the Area Traffic Commissioners who became Regional Traffic Commissioners, the man in charge of the North Western Region being Sir William Chamberlain, Oldham's former General Manager from 1918 to 1925.

Some months previously the Traffic Commissioner had instructed all bus operators to prepare contingency plans designed to save 50% of the fuel they were then using, while maintaining a full service for workmen. So, from 24th September 1939 all frequencies were reduced and some were suspended altogether between the peaks on weekdays, although after an appeal to the Traffic Commissioner the Transport Department was able to get a supplementary allocation of fuel enabling some of the cuts to be restored on 22nd November. However, the Commissioner ruled that all services should leave the town centre no later than 10pm. But these draconian cuts were to a degree offset by the steady influx of the new buses already on order for the proposed tram conversions which enabled as many single-deck workings as possible to be converted to double-deck operation.

At the beginning of the war Oldham Corporation was running the following services:

A	Chapel Road-Oldham-Greenacres
B	Derker-Oldham-Booth Hill
C	Star Inn-Middleton Junction
D	Rhodes Bank-Long Lane
E	Oldham-Mossley
F	Shaw-Royton-Middleton
G	Oldham-Abbey Hills
H	Oldham-Denshaw
M	Summit-Oldham-Hathershaw
N	Oldham-Stalybridge
O	Hollinwood-Oldham-Grotton
P	Oldham-Uppermill circular
V	Glodwick circular
1	* Waterhead-Oldham-Hollinwood
2	Newhey-Shaw-Royton-Manchester
3	Shaw-Oldham-Middleton
4	Glodwick circular
5	Grains Bar-Oldham-Burnley Lane
6	Moorside-Oldham-Burnley Lane
7	Higginshaw-Oldham-Chadderton
8	* Shaw-Royton-Hollinwood
9	Rochdale-Oldham-Ashton
10	Greenfield-Oldham-Manchester
13	Uppermill-Oldham-Manchester
14	Uppermill-Oldham-Manchester
20	* Waterhead-Oldham-Manchester
59	Shaw-Oldham-Middleton-Manchester

* *Tram services, the remainder buses.*

Two tram services were still running at the outbreak of war; 1/20 Waterhead-Oldham-Hollinwood-Manchester and 8 Shaw-Royton-Hollinwood still remaining to be converted. Due to the poor condition of the former steam tramway track along Featherstall Road the Regional Traffic Commissioner granted a Wartime Permit for this conversion to take place once sufficient new vehicles had been delivered, the last tram on the route running on 2nd December 1939. With fuel shortages beginning to bite services 1 and 20 would remain for the duration of hostilities.

From the end of the year all employees were paid a War Wage, an additional payment of up to four shillings a week depending on age. Blackout conditions and fuel rationing, combined to present the Transport Department with a host of difficulties but at the beginning of 1940 these were exacerbated by the weather. A period of frost and severe blizzards which was the worst for many years hit the area at the end of January; Oldham being particularly vulnerable due to the hilly and often exposed nature of its routes. Saddleworth was completely cut off for a week and many other services could not run their full length for several days.

Service D was extended to the Gardeners Arms at New Moston in February 1940, mainly to carry workers to and from AV Roe's aircraft factory on Greengate where some 18,000 people, mainly women, were building sections of Lancaster bombers which were then taken to Woodford for assembly and flight testing. Manchester's 56 service, which ran in Oldham's operating area between Owler Lane, Chadderton and Hollinwood Station, and on which Oldham held a joint licence, had been an early victim of the wartime economies but some journeys were quickly reinstated at shift times to serve AV Roe and Ferranti. Service 3 was cut back from Middleton to Mills Hill and service 5 was turned short at Westhulme Avenue.

Circulars from the Ministry of War Transport were coming out thick and fast. One raised the permissible laden weight of double-deckers from 10½ tons to 11 tons 'in view of the fact that that the use of alternative materials due to war conditions was likely to increase the weight of the vehicles'. Then the *War Transport (Standing Passengers) Order* raised the maximum standing passengers to 30 on single-deck buses 'with alternative seating arrangements'. Fourteen single-deckers, Leyland TS3s 59-62 and TS4s 63 and 21-29 were converted to standees with perimeter seating for 30, an official maximum of 60 passengers which in practice would often be exceeded. The *War Transport (Standing Passengers) No.2 Order* followed shortly, raising the maximum permitted standing passengers on unmodified single-deckers and in the lower saloons of double-deckers to twelve, resulting in the unfortunate conductor having difficulty in collecting fares during the blackout as well as supervising the platform. To counter this the fitting of honesty boxes was considered but rejected.

The solution, as in some other undertakings, was to employ auxiliary conductors. These were regular travellers who were willing to ride on the platform, ring the bell to stop and start the bus, and announce the name of the stop, but were not responsible for collecting fares. For this they were allowed to travel free on the journey concerned. In the early days of the war bus driving was not yet a reserved occupation and the conscription of employees for military service was creating a labour shortage. Having considered various options it was decided in January 1940 to employ women conductors as a temporary expedient but, unlike in some neighbouring undertakings, many stayed on well after the war ended. The women were paid a maximum wage of £2 a week, the same amount paid to women in other war services.

Workshops and factories were instructed to stagger their working hours and in Oldham, consultation between the Transport Department and the employers resulted in the starting and finishing times being brought earlier from the end of the year. This made better use of the available daylight and also enabled buses to be saved which could then be used to strengthen services elsewhere.

New Roe-bodied Leyland TD5s were still being delivered from the 180-226 order but the Ministry would only issue permits for 20, their intention being to divert the remainder elsewhere. However, in May 1940 Oldham were asked to loan buses to Liverpool Corporation and a deal was struck whereby the new buses would come to Oldham and older ones would be loaned out instead. Liverpool had by now made other arrangements, so Oldham loaned the buses to other operators who had lost vehicles in air raids, or needed more vehicles to run extra services for munitions factories. In all a total of 31 buses were hired out, 14 to Red and White, 12 to Bristol Tramways and 5 to Lancashire United.

Still optimistic about the length of the war, and no doubt with an eye to being at the front of the queue when hostilities eventually ended, the Corporation placed provisional orders for 14 Leyland double-deckers and 21 Daimler single-deckers to replace vehicles which would normally have become time-expired during the next couple of years. New bus production, however, was now limited to Daimler and Guy and these were supplied under the *Acquisition and Disposal of Motor Vehicles Order* on permits issued by the Regional Traffic Commissioner. As new buses were still being delivered to Oldham the permits were refused; the Daimlers never materialised and Leyland, fully committed to the production of tanks and other military vehicles, put the order in the pending tray. The buses eventually arrived as the post-war model PD1 in 1946 and meanwhile the older buses had to soldier on.

During October 1940 a comprehensive scheme for mutual aid was drawn up between 30 municipal undertakings and four companies in the region, agreement being reached on the pooling of garage accommodation and inter-fleet hiring of buses in the event of any of the operators suffering damage by enemy air raids. With the big engineering firms turning over to production of munitions, Oldham became a target for enemy bombing raids from an early date and during late 1940 the Belgium Mill on Blackshaw Lane, Royton was destroyed and a cluster of incendiaries fell on the Derker housing estate. Early in 1941 a string of 25 bombs intended for Platts and Ferranti was dropped across Hollinwood and the Coppice.

During 1941 1933 Roe-bodied Leyland TS4 number 24 (BU 7611) was converted to run on town gas which was carried in a bag on the roof. As with other such experiments it was short-lived and the bag was soon removed. ***(STA)***

To minimise the risk of losing much of the fleet in one attack, as had happened elsewhere in the country, Oldham began to disperse its buses, parking them overnight and between the peaks in smaller numbers away from the town centre. Two locations were used, a recreation ground on Rochdale Road and a coal storage site on Chamber Road, some 80 buses being involved. In the event Oldham did not lose any buses to enemy action.

The darkest hour

The loss of Burma and Malaya to the Japanese in 1942 cut off supplies of rubber and led to a further tightening of belts. The Regional Traffic Commissioner first instructed all operators to bring forward the departure time of last buses from town centres to 10pm, but later in the year he demanded more drastic reductions to achieve a further 10% saving in mileage, while retaining the full workmen's services. Oldham's services were again reduced in frequency; last journeys left the town centre about 9pm and Sunday services did not run before 2pm.

By now the cuts were really starting to hurt and there were many complaints of overcrowding and passengers being left behind throughout the system. The Sunday cuts attracted vociferous opposition, especially from the churches, but any reinstatement was flatly rejected.

Sickness among drivers and conductors had risen to more than twice the level before the war, and much of it was attributed to the continual strain of driving in the blackout or trying to collect fares on packed buses in virtual darkness. There was also a shortage of crimson paint so it was decided to paint older buses grey if and when required.

With the continuing shortage of fuel, the Government instructed all larger operators with over 100 vehicles to convert 10% of their fleet to use Producer Gas. Oldham's target was 18 buses but the work went slowly and in the end only four buses were converted, petrol-engined single-deckers 63 and 65 and diesel-engined double-deckers 80 and 128. The coke-fired gas

The year is 1942 and although it is not specifically to do with the war this photograph of Leyland TD5 number 166 (ABU 384), embedded in a shop front in George Street, provides an opportunity to show the dark grey roof all buses acquired as wartime camouflage. ***(MMT)***

Below
Oldham's share of the Yelloway operation purchased jointly with Manchester and Rochdale in 1944 was this all-Leyland TD5 DDK 256 which had been new to Yelloway in 1938. It became number 227 in the Oldham fleet but retained its original destination layout until withdrawal in 1952. ***(STA)***

plant produced fumes which, when mixed with water vapour formed a gas, which could then be mixed with petrol or diesel fuel in the cylinders. It reduced the engine's power by about a third and was impractical on hilly routes which in Oldham restricted its use somewhat. The gas plant was mounted on a trailer towed behind the bus, which also precluded its use on any route involving a reverse. The single-deckers were restricted to service E (Mossley) which was not exactly flat and on more than one occasion a bus would stall on the steep climb of Salem Brow from Lees Brook up to Clarksfield Road and would have to be towed the rest of the way. The double-deckers were used on services D (New Moston) and 4/V (Glodwick Circular). The experiment was not a success and was abandoned with some relief in September 1944.

Following a string of complaints of poor connections between Rochdale and Oldham buses at Thornham Summit, the two services were linked to run through between Rochdale and Hathershaw from 19th December 1943. Other service changes during the war involved alternate journeys to Grotton being cut back to County End, buses then showing O to County End and T to Grotton, while the short workings between Heron Street and Clarksfield Road became S.

Light at the end of the tunnel

The German retreat on all fronts culminating in the D-Day landings in France in June 1944 reversed the fortunes of the war. The Allies were now winning and a new spirit of optimism was apparent.

In general, long distance coach services, particularly those aimed at the holiday market, had been suspended during the war. For operators like Yelloway, whose business relied heavily on this type of traffic, the effect had been little short of a disaster. Faced with a need for finance to keep the business afloat until normal services could be resumed, Yelloway approached Manchester, Oldham and Rochdale Corporations in January 1944 with a view to them buying the Rochdale-Royton-Manchester express service and after lengthy negotiations the sale was agreed at a price of £38,500, Oldham's share being £16,651. The service was taken over on 18th June 1944 and Oldham was allocated one all-day working on the route which was given the number 24. This was not used by either Oldham or Rochdale, but caused Manchester to renumber its Cheetham Hill to Moston route from 24 to 26. With the service came three buses. The first was a Leyland-bodied Titan TD5, dating from 1938, which duly became 227 (DDK 256). It was fitted out to a high specification with comfortable seats and a folding door between the platform and the lower saloon as befitted a luxury coach operator. It was intended to alter the blind layout to Oldham's standard and instead a special short blind was made up to cover services N and 24 on which it worked for the rest of its life. There were also two Burlingham-bodied Leyland Tiger TS1 full coaches, DK 7378 and DK 7379 dating from 1931, which were sold to a Leicestershire coach operator without being used in Oldham.

In September 1944, with the end of enemy air raids, blackout restrictions were eased on the main roads and in the town centre and in November the Regional Traffic Commissioner relaxed the curfew and allowed last buses to leave the town termini at 10pm, instead of 9pm as they had done for over two years. On 9th May 1945 the war ended in Europe. Overnight the masks over the headlights and saloon lighting were removed, the white patches on the mudguards and rear corners were quickly painted out, and a semblance of normality returned.

7 – THE POST-WAR YEARS

Co-ordination and Nationalisation

The euphoria that came with the Allied victory in Europe did not last long, however. The war was still going on in the Far East and there were shortages and rationing at home, so things did not change very much in practical terms for the average Oldham resident. As in 1918 there was a need to concentrate scarce resources on rebuilding the neglected and worn out infrastructure, there were arrears of maintenance and a shortage of spare parts and many of the Department's employees were still away in the armed forces. Perversely, after years of restrictions demand for travel was booming.

Once more co-ordination was in the air and on 20th June 1945 the Municipal Passenger Transport Association convened a conference in Manchester, attended by representatives from all the municipal transport operators in the area, to consider how best to secure this in the planning of post-war passenger services, particularly in regard to future satellite towns, new housing estates and new industries. A Joint Transport Advisory Group was set up consisting of representatives of Ashton-under-Lyne, Bolton, Bury, Manchester, Oldham, Rochdale, Salford and Stockport Corporations and the SHMD Board.

At the General Election on 5th July 1945, Clement Attlee's left wing Labour government, committed to the nationalisation of all means of production and distribution, was elected with a large majority. This sent shock waves throughout the transport industry, although municipal undertakings, being already in public ownership, did not at first foresee a problem, wrongly assuming that nationalisation would only apply to private companies. However, as details of the draft Transport Bill came out, it became clear that its scope was to be far wider reaching than had been anticipated.

The Bill proposed the establishment of a British Transport Commission mandated to provide an adequate, economical and integrated system of transport, and included the transfer of all undertakings operating passenger transport services to a number of Area Transport Boards. Oldham, like other municipalities in the area, had been happy to consider voluntary co-ordination of certain conditions, but there was no way it would willingly give up control of its transport undertaking. Its philosophy was that local control of local services, including passenger transport, was essential to the development of the town, that control should be in the hands of elected representatives and any area boards should comprise members chosen from the elected representatives of the area. Feelings ran high and representations were made to the Government and it did not help much when the newly-formed Road Passenger Transport Executive replied that as it had no legal duty to consult the authorities concerned, it did not think that any useful purpose would be served by inviting representations. The Government was not to be swayed and the Bill subsequently became the Road Traffic Act, 1947, becoming law on 1st January 1948.

Despite the passing of the Act, the South East Lancashire and East Cheshire Municipal Passenger Transport Association Joint Advisory Group continued to meet regularly in an attempt to standardise conditions of workmen's and children's fares, carriage of dogs and parcels, half fare computations and the like, but could never get agreement between the constituent operators and, in the face of more pressing matters, interest declined until eventually the committee was disbanded.

Although nationalisation of the private bus companies happened fairly quickly, the draft proposals for a Northern Area Transport Board were not published until October 1949. Shortly afterwards, on 23rd February 1950, a further General Election resulted in the government being returned with an unworkably small majority. Faced with mounting unpopularity among a population that had endured a period of austerity and rationing as long as the war itself, the government again went to the country and on 25th October 1951 they were swept from power. While nationalisation remained, the scheme for area boards was quietly dropped, not to be resurrected until the plans for Conurbation Transport Executives some 15 years later.

Getting restarted

Away from the national scene there was still a need to get on with running the job at a local level. Sunday morning services were reinstated in July 1945, and during the year the use of auxiliary conductors came to an end and the temporary standing arrangements ceased. Things were starting to return to normal.

The Ministry of Transport stopped issuing licences for the purchase and disposal of vehicles from 1st January 1946. Now every operator wanted new buses to replace worn out vehicles and to increase their fleets to cater for the explosion in demand, but the government's '*Export or die*' policy was that exports must come first to pay off the huge war debt. Oldham's orders that had been refused by the Government four years earlier were increased by another 120 to a total of 134 buses, all but ten with Roe bodies, but due to the long waiting list the last ones were not delivered until 1950.

The first 14 (228-41), which had been provisionally ordered during the war, began to arrive in July 1946 as the new Leyland PD1 model carrying somewhat Spartan Roe bodies without saloon heaters and were known in Oldham as 'Utilities'. The bodies were basically the same as Roe's pre-war version fitted to the TD5 chassis, outwardly the noticeable differences being the substitution of sliding ventilators for the half-drop windows and the offside destination replaced by a service number. As crimson lake paint was in short supply after the war the buses came in a bright red colour. They were fitted with the new Leyland 7.4 litre E.181 engine and a very slow-changing crash-gearbox resulting in low gear having to be held for an excessive time on the long uphill gradients. To counter this, a clutch stop was fitted which slowed the engine when the clutch was fully depressed enabling a fast change to be made, but it was unreliable and many drivers continued to double declutch.

These first post-war buses were 7ft 6in wide, but later, when the maximum gross weight was lifted to 12 tons and the permitted width was increased to 8ft, all subsequent deliveries were built to the new standards. Suitable routes had to be agreed with the police for 8ft wide operation and the list eventually authorised by the Traffic Commissioner generally comprised the main roads, all other routes remaining at the old limit until the restriction was removed completely in 1950.

The new arrivals were used to implement the conversion of the sole remaining tram route between Waterhead and Manchester.

Oldham's first post-war buses were a batch of 14 Leyland Titan PD1s with bodywork by Roe developed from their immediate pre-war design with detail differences such as the sliding window vents on both decks. Number 235 (DBU 27) is pictured at the Roe factory in 1946 before delivery in its temporary red livery with painted radiator shell. ***(STA)***

Oldham was quick to take advantage of the new regulations permitting 8ft wide buses and in 1947 took delivery of 25 Roe-bodied Leyland Titan PD1/3 models, the wider version of the PD1. Number 252 (DBU 252) is pictured on Union Street on service G to Abbey Hills. ***(MMT)***

A further 25 identical buses arrived the following year. Number 279 (DBU 279) tackles the steep climb up Rochdale Road out of Shaw while working a journey on service F from Shaw to Royton, normally a single-deck operation. ***(JJH)***

Originally planned to take place in June 1946, its implementation was twice delayed due to the slow delivery of the new buses. The last tram eventually ran on 3rd August and buses took over the following day on the replacement 98 service between Waterhead and Manchester (Stevenson Square). Like the trams it was jointly operated with Manchester Corporation which turned out brand new Crossleys from Hyde Road Garage to work the route. Supplementary journeys between Waterhead and Hollinwood were run solely by Oldham, retaining service number 1. As more buses were delivered their use was extended to the long 59 route and the express services.

The first 8ft buses were 50 Leyland PD1/3 models also with Roe bodies but reverting to pre-war standards with saloon heaters and moquette upholstered seats. These buses had a board in the cab saying "8ft wide. To be used only on authorised routes." They were delivered in two batches, 242-66 in 1947 and 267-91 in 1948. Number 244 was in fact the first 8ft wide bus built by Leyland. Number 246 lasted long enough to become SELNEC's 5246 in 1969, passing into preservation the following year. Meanwhile, still desperate for serviceable buses and also short of manpower in the workshops, it was proposed to re-body the 21 Leyland TD5s 132-52, whose English Electric bodies were giving cause for concern. In the end only twelve buses, were rebuilt, seven (132/3/5-8/40) by Samlesbury Engineering Ltd of Blackburn and five (143/6/8-50) by the now forgotten local firm of M Hearn Ltd. Number 152 received a lesser refurbishment in the Wallshaw Street workshops, but nevertheless was withdrawn with the un-rebuilt buses in 1950 and lay derelict in the yard for some time as a source of spares.

More growth

The continuing shortage of buses was generally, at least in the beginning, the result of difficulty in maintaining the fleet during the war. There were other contributory factors however; not least the construction of new housing estates on the outskirts of the town. Improved expectations in living standards and public hygiene saw the demolition of closely packed back to back houses near to the town centre and their replacement by new estates of lower density housing on the edge of the town nearer to the open fields and moors. Although this was a great step forward in social terms, it meant that fewer passengers were being carried longer distances at greater cost.

There was also a shortage of conductors as many employees were still in the armed forces, or had opted not to return to their former positions, instead choosing better paid jobs and conditions in other industries. So conductresses, engaged during the war as a temporary expedient, stayed on, some for many years. They were not allowed to become drivers, however, as in those days driving was considered to be a man's job, which it probably was then in view of the heavy steering and brakes of contemporary buses. It used to be said that you could always tell a bus driver by the size of his calf muscles.

Coming on top of these ongoing problems, the 1947 winter was one of the harshest in living memory, the Oldham area being gripped by blizzards with winds blowing relentless snow from the east and continuing for days. In Saddleworth there were drifts up to 14 feet high and snow remained on the ground in some places until May!

To cater for changes in traffic flows resulting from new housing developments at Stottfield to the west of Royton town centre, at Shore Edge above Shaw and at Belgrave Road at Hathershaw, some services were reorganised during 1948. On 18th July service B (Derker-Market Place-Booth Hill was extended through Royton, and Mills Hill to Middleton as service 12, with alternate short journeys to Stottfield numbered 11. Service F (Shaw-Royton-Mills Hill-Middleton) lost its Royton to Middleton section, but was extended at the Shaw end along Milnrow Road and up Buckstones Road to Shore Edge. Crossley single-decker 300 worked the first day's service to Shore Edge carrying a floral wreath on its radiator, a little touch which was to be repeated a few years later when service C was extended to Strinesdale. Finally, a new service B was introduced between Belgrave Road and Middleton Junction via Honeywell Lane, Ashton Road, King Street, Manchester Street, Werneth, Edward Street, Fields New Road and Foxdenton Lane. Being double-deck operated, buses turned at Middleton Junction by reversing into Junction Street, just before the lift bridge over the Rochdale Canal and the low railway bridge.

Also during 1948 requests were received for

limited stop journeys on the former Yelloway service 24 from Rochdale to Manchester via Royton, now jointly operated by Oldham, Manchester and Rochdale Corporations. Oldham drew up a scheme to divert the service via Chadderton Town Hall putting an extra four minutes on the running time, but at the same time introducing a peak hour express service (90) observing service 24 stops between Rochdale and Royton, then non-stop to Manchester (Stevenson Square). The revisions to service 24 did not come into operation until Sunday 1st May 1949 with the express service starting the following morning, the delay being due to protracted negotiations on the inter-availability of return tickets between service 90 and the parallel Manchester, Oldham and North Western Road Car operated service 2 between Royton and Manchester.

New house building continued steadily and on 12th March 1950 service 7, which had for several years supplemented 3 and 59 between Chadderton and Higginshaw was diverted off Middleton Road via Manchester Road, Chapel Road and Limeside Road to serve a new estate at Limeside south of Hollins Road. Then two weeks later on 26th March service C Middleton Junction-Rhodes Bank was extended along Ripponden Road to Moorside and up Turf Pit Lane to Strinesdale, a small council estate a thousand feet above sea level on the windswept moors completed nearly three years earlier but which until that time had not had an access road suitable for buses. Some years later Oldham Council moved the residents out and sold the estate to a private property company which upgraded the houses and renamed it Pennine Meadows.

When these changes had been made the network assumed the shape that, with a few minor amendments, was to last for the next twenty years. The services then operated were:-

A Chapel Road-Oldham-Greenacres
B Belgrave Road-Oldham-Middleton Junc.
C Strinesdale-Middleton Junction
D Rhodes Bank-New Moston
E Oldham-Mossley
F Royton-Shaw-Shore Edge
G Oldham-Abbey Hills
H Oldham-Denshaw
M Summit-Oldham-Hathershaw
N Oldham-Stalybridge
O Hollinwood-Oldham-Lees
P Oldham-Uppermill circular
S Heron St-Oldham-Clarksfield Road
T Hollinwood-Oldham-Grotton
V Glodwick clockwise circular
1 Waterhead-Oldham-Hollinwood
2 Newhey-Shaw-Royton-Manchester
3 Shaw-Oldham-Mills Hill
4 Glodwick anti-clockwise circular
5 Grains Bar-Oldham-Burnley Lane
6 Moorside-Oldham-Burnley Lane
7 Higginshaw-Oldham-Limeside
8 Shaw-Royton-Hollinwood
9 Rochdale-Oldham-Ashton
10 Greenfield-Oldham-Manchester
11 Derker-Oldham-Royton-Stottfield
12 Derker-Oldham-Royton-Middleton
13 Uppermill-Oldham-Manchester
14 Uppermill-Oldham-Manchester
20 Waterhead-Oldham-Manchester
24 Rochdale-Royton- Manchester
34 Oldham-Manchester express
59 Shaw-Oldham-Middleton-Manchester
90 Rochdale-Royton-Manchester express

New buses

The remaining 70 of the order for 134 buses followed quickly. First came ten Crossley SD42/3 models numbered 292-301 with single-deck bodies by Roe which arrived during 1948 and enabled the 1931 and 1932 Tigers to be withdrawn. Only a handful of pre-war single-deckers now remained in service, notable among which were the three full-fronted TS6s bought in 1934 for the express services.

These were followed by a further ten Crossleys, 302-11, this time the DD42 model, Crossley's standard post-war double-deck chassis developed from the 1944 prototype which was running in Manchester. Oldham always referred to these buses as 42/5 but that was a 7ft 6in bus which was in widespread use among neighbouring undertakings and elsewhere and Oldham's were more likely to have been the 42/4 which was the 8ft equivalent. Visually, these buses were pleasing on the eye with a low bonnet, deep cab windows and a distinctive body style built by Crossley to Manchester's streamline specification which featured a raised lower edge to the last two windows on either side of both decks. Towards

In 1948 Oldham ordered ten Crossley SD42/3 models with Roe single-deck bodies to replace early Leyland Tigers that had soldiered on through the war and its aftermath. Number 293 (DBU 293) is pictured at the Roe factory before delivery. ***(STA)***

the end of the war Manchester had developed a method of cantilevering the rear platform from the main body frame rather than bolting a sub frame on to the chassis as, in a collision, this reduced potential damage to the chassis frames and therefore time out of service and the cost of repairs. Consequently, the upper deck incorporated additional strengthening resulting in the smaller windows and the lower deck was treated in the same way to match. Crossley adopted the design as standard for some time, even on buses with conventionally constructed platforms although it was subsequently dropped. Good looking they may have been, but this was little consolation to drivers who struggled to keep time with heavy loads, while battling with low power, a difficult constant mesh gearbox and heavy steering, often having to stand up to get the bus around tight corners at low speeds.

Next came 312-36, 25 Daimler CVD6s with Daimler engines and pre-selector gearboxes. The original body order had gone to Crossley but due to a problem with delivery dates at the Errwood Park factory 312-21 were eventually bodied by Roe.

The final buses in the order were 25 Leyland PD2/3s numbered 337-61, also with Roe bodies. These were a development of the PD1 with the new and more powerful 9.8 litre O.600 engine and a syncromesh gearbox which made them a favourite with drivers. The first bus of the batch, number 337, was displayed on the Roe stand at the 1948 Commercial Motor Show at Earls Court. The show model had fluorescent lights that were soon removed and no offside service number box which was to become a standard feature on all later models after 1950.

Another small order for eight Crossleys followed soon after. These were four SD42/7 single-deckers with Roe bodies numbered 362-65 and four DD42/8 double-deckers with Crossley bodies numbered 366-69. Outwardly, the only differences from the previous models from the same manufacturer were the substitution of the Crossley name for the Maltese Cross emblem on the radiators and the polished chrome radiator shells on the four double-deckers. But hidden from view under the bonnet was an improved engine developed after Crossley's acquisition by AEC and a syncromesh gearbox. However, the syncromesh was not as efficient as that on the Leylands and drivers would still double declutch for a faster gear change.

Now that the wartime backlog had been made good and allowance made for post-war expansion the fleet was to remain virtually static for the next five years.

In the immediate post-war period Leyland Motors had a full order book and there was a long wait for deliveries. Consequently Oldham, with an urgent need for new buses, was forced to split its orders and as well as the Crossleys 25 Daimler CVD6s came into the fleet, the only ones in the post-war era. Roe-bodied number 312 (EBU 912), the first to be delivered is pictured on High Street on its way to Lees on service O. ***(MMT)***

The 1950 deliveries included 25 of the new Leyland PD2 models with syncromesh gearboxes much to the relief of the drivers. These were long-lived buses, some lasting into PTE days. Number 347 (EBU 877) is seen at the Stottfield terminus at Royton while working on service 11. ***(AM)***

Number 365 (FBU824) was the last of four Crossley SD42/7 chassis fitted with Crossley bodies which were delivered in 1950 and saw off the last of the pre-war single-deckers. It is pictured in the depot yard at Wallshaw Street. Note the generally more solid appearance than Roe-bodied number 293. ***(STA)***

The last non-Leyland buses in the Oldham fleet were four Crossley DD42/8s with Crossley bodies which arrived in 1950. Now preserved, number 368 (FBU 827), is pictured parked in the Wallshaw Street depot alongside similarly-bodied Daimler CVD6 number 327 (EBU 927). ***(MMT)***

8 – THE FRUGAL FIFTIES

Financial problems

The decade of the fifties signalled the beginning of a long period of falling patronage and rising costs. It started with bus operators at a low point with their fleets still largely run down from the war and a lengthy wait for new bus orders to be delivered. There was still rationing and Government control of just about everything they needed to rebuild their business and it is interesting to conjecture what might have been if the industry had been able to respond quickly and adequately to the immediate post-war desire for travel. However, by the time new buses started coming into service the boom was over and competition from television and the private car was already making inroads into passenger levels.

In a labour intensive industry such as bus operation costs soared out of all proportion to those in manufacturing which was rapidly becoming more and more automated. Service cuts were not acceptable so the only option left was to raise fares, and regular above-inflation increases during the 1950s only worsened comparisons with the car. Every little bit of extra revenue counted and one way was external advertising on the buses. While not being happy with the idea the Committee took the pragmatic decision to go ahead, even agreeing to advertising alcoholic drinks and football pools! The adverts began to appear on bus sides from the end of 1953.

One way to reduce labour costs was increased mechanisation in the depot and workshops and to this end towards the end of 1954 Mr Paige proposed to obtain a Dawson automatic bus washing machine. The committee agreed and it was purchased for £2,847, plus £200 for fitting and a further £600 for ancillary works, this amount being offset by a saving of 11 cleaners.

Until now Oldham, like most other municipal operators, had followed the time-honoured practice of issuing tickets from a hand-held rack cancelled by the conductor with a punch which clipped out the relevant stages. However, at the beginning of 1950 it was decided to hire a number of 'Ultimate' ticket dispensing machines from their manufacturer, the Bell Punch Company, for use on local services. Initially, 150 five-barrel models were obtained, which held five rolls of pre-printed tickets issued by pressing down a lever on the front of the machine. By careful selection of values and issuing tickets in specific combinations it was possible to cover most fares with only two tickets. Later machines were of the six-barrel variety which allowed higher fares to be issued. However, as the longer distance joint services had considerably higher fares including returns, special punched tickets continued in use until they were eventually replaced by TIM machines, of which 11 were bought. Ten were later used on OMO routes with an electric base, the other one being allocated to Conductor Bert Harrop who had lost part of his thumb and couldn't operate an Ultimate.

Celebrations were in order in 1950 when Oldham marked the 50th anniversary of the opening of its first electric tramway on 15th December 1900. A dinner was organised and a commemorative brochure was produced. The general gloom was gradually lifting and the Festival of Britain on London's South Bank in the summer of 1951, followed by the Coronation of the young Queen Elizabeth II on 2nd June 1953, heralded a period of optimism; the new Elizabethan age, the latter being marked by decorating the depot and town centre premises.

Fine-tuning

By now the route network had virtually reached its maximum extent and all that remained was a little fine-tuning, mainly to serve new housing developments. During 1952 Royton Council asked for a more direct and faster service to Manchester throughout the day. So, Oldham proposed to abandon the Chadderton loop on service 24 which had been introduced some three years previously and revert to the direct route along Broadway which had previously been operated since Yelloway days. Rochdale and Manchester, not being directly concerned, went along with the proposal and backed the application. There was a predictable reaction from Chadderton Council and its residents, and the Traffic Commissioner refused to grant it.

At the same time Crompton Council were building a new housing estate at Rushcroft and early in 1953 service 3 was extended from the Wren's Nest to serve it.

For several years Lees Council had been agitating for a service along Stamford Road to Waterhead but Oldham had always considered it not viable and had rejected it. However, it was eventually agreed to divert some County End journeys on service O for a trial period, but the police objected on the grounds that the roads, especially the junction with Lees High Street, were unsuitable. When the necessary road widening took place a service was eventually introduced as far as Hey Crescent. There were repeated requests for a further extension to Huddersfield Road and Waterhead, returning to Oldham as a circular route, but it would be many years, after de-regulation, before such a service materialised. Then, to serve a new estate at Fitton Hill to the east of Ashton Road, service B was extended a short distance from its Belgrave Road terminus along Keswick Avenue and Fir Tree Avenue to Fitton Hill Community Centre on 16th July 1953.

The following year another new housing estate was completed at Holts, a mile beyond the Abbey Hills terminus and only served on its edge by the hourly route N between Oldham and Stalybridge. To cater for the increased demand a new service 20 started running into the estate on 15th September 1954 following the same route as service G from the Town Hall along Waterloo Street and Abbey Hills Road. This service was essentially temporary and as the estate grew the route pattern was modified. Less than twelve months later 20 was withdrawn and G and 7 were combined, G becoming Limeside to Holts and 7 Holts to Limeside. The use of separate service letters/numbers in opposite directions was unusual but not unique as a method of identifying the outer terminus on cross-town services. Eventually, on 17th April 1959 the services were further revised with G and 7 cut back from Holts to Abbey Hills and 4 and V extended to Holts instead.

In the meantime, in order to reduce costs and tailor capacity to the traffic on offer, there was a restructuring and simplifying of the Ripponden Road route. On 8th September 1957 former tram services 5 (Westhulme Avenue to Grains Bar) and 6 (Burnley Lane-Moorside), which had run unchanged for nearly thirty years, were extended to Denshaw and Strinesdale respectively. As a result H (Market Place-Denshaw) was withdrawn and C (Middleton Junction-Strinesdale) was taken off Ripponden Road and diverted along Henshaw Street to a new terminus at Bar Gap Road, a few yards from the site of Oldham's former Oldham Edge bus depot.

Before 1954 bus routes through Oldham town centre were quite simple, all buses going straight along High Street, Yorkshire Street and Mumps or via Union Street in both directions. Then on 19th September all outward journeys were diverted along Wallshaw Place, better known as 'The Grotto', past the front of the depot to relieve the growing traffic congestion caused by crew

In 1952 a small order for three buses was delivered. These were Leyland Titan PD2/12s with Leyland bodies of which number 370 (HBU 123), the first of the trio, is pictured here working on service 59 between Shaw and Manchester. ***(MMT)***

The 1953 order for new buses comprised 15 Leyland PD2/20s, five bodied by Metro-Cammell and ten by Roe. Number 373 (KBU 383), which arrived in 1955, was numerically the first of the batch and carried an ultra-lightweight Metro-Cammell body. It is pictured above leaving Stevenson Square, Manchester on the peak period express service 90 to Rochdale. The bus behind is number 389 (NBU 489), a 1957 Roe-bodied Leyland bound for Newhey on service 2. ***(JJH)***

In the middle picture similar vehicle 375 (KBU 385) drops down from Thornham Summit on a service 9 journey from Oldham to Rochdale. ***(STA)***

Number 384 (KBU 379) poses for the photographer in the Mumps lay-by. ***(JJH)***

changes on the main A62 trunk road. Three years later on 26th April 1957 another small scheme was introduced with inward buses from Mumps travelling along Union Street and regaining Yorkshire Street by Waterloo Street.

More new buses

With fleet replacement complete for the time being the early part of the decade was a quiet period with very few new buses being purchased. A small order for three Leyland double-deckers arrived in 1952. These were the PD2/12 model which was a slightly longer version of the PD2/3 to take advantage of the changed regulations which had increased the maximum permitted length to 27ft a couple of years earlier. In a new departure for Oldham they carried standard Leyland metal framed bodies which would be the only new post-war examples of that manufacturer's bodywork in the fleet as Leyland were to cease building bus bodies shortly afterwards. There were still some hundred or so pre-war buses running but most of these would have to soldier on for a few years yet.

At this time, with the relentless increase in the price of diesel, manufacturers were turning their attention to improving fuel consumption. One way to achieve this was to reduce the weight of both chassis and bodies. By dispensing with much of the inner skin and using aluminium alloy wherever it could, the MCW group produced an ultra light body in time to be displayed at the 1952 Commercial Motor Show. Known as the 'Orion', when mated with a lightweight chassis, it tipped the scales at 6ton 2cwt, considerably less than the eight tons of a Crossley of a few years earlier. Production vehicles were a little heavier, however. Looking for 15 new buses the Transport Committee travelled to Birmingham to visit the Metropolitan-Cammell works and the members were impressed enough by what they saw to order five of these bodies, although they hedged their bets by awarding the rest of the contract to Roe. The buses were the new Leyland PD2/20 model with the full-width 'tin' front pioneered by Midland Red. The ten Roe-bodied buses (378-87) arrived in September 1954 with the five Orions following at the end of the year. The Orions were ungainly looking vehicles, the slight taper of the upper deck giving rise to various names such as 'loaf tins' and 'spam cans' and the lightweight construction resulted in vibrating panels and a bouncy ride.

Soon after these buses were delivered orders were placed for another 31 buses, more Leyland PD2/20s with the body order split between Roe (20), Park Royal (5) and Northern Counties (6). Park Royal sub-contracted its part of the order to Crossley. All 31 buses arrived during 1957 as 388-418.

In 1958 Roe-bodied Leyland Titan TD5 209 was de-roofed under the low bridge at Hollinwood station and converted to a breakdown tender. Known as 'Red Biddy' it gave several years more service in that form.

Finally, to replace the remaining pre-war vehicles, a further 44 Leylands were ordered. These were the PD2/30 model; the bodies again split three ways, this time between Metro-Cammell (10), Roe (24) and Northern Counties (10). All were of semi-lightweight construction using aluminium extensively on the upper decks, but lessons had been learned and none went to such extremes as the original five Orions. These buses were to be the last new open rear platform examples in the fleet and when delivery was complete in 1959 all the remaining pre-war vehicles had gone, the oldest buses were 13 years old and the average age was a little over seven years.

But big changes in bus design were in the offing. Bristol's Lodekka with its revolutionary drop axle had swept away the inconvenient side gangways of lowbridge models, but with no low bridges other than the ultra-low one at Middleton Junction, Oldham did not need low-height buses. However, the department still had green-painted AEC/Park Royal Bridgemaster 116 TMD demonstrator on loan for a week in April 1959. But of more interest was Leyland's Atlantean which, with its rear-mounted engine and the platform next to the driver ahead of the front wheel, would change the whole face of bus operation for ever.

So as the fifties slipped into the sixties momentous changes were ahead and Oldham Corporation would enter its final decade.

A further 31 buses ordered in 1955 were all delivered during 1957. They were more Leyland PD2/20s, the body order being divided three ways between Roe, Crossley and Northern Counties. One of the five Northern Counties-bodied buses, number 417 (NBU 517), is pictured above, posing for its official photograph. ***(JJH)***

In the upper picture on the opposite page, number 405 (NBU 505) with traditional Roe body stands outside the Roe works before delivery. It became SELNEC 5305 and was withdrawn in 1973. ***(STA)***

Number 411 (NBU 511), a Crossley-bodied variant, crosses King Street into Union Street West on its way to Chapel Road on service A while an empty Foden 8-wheel tipper belonging to Eldon Hill Quarries turns left towards Ashton on its way back to Buxton for another load of stone. ***(MMT)***

OLDHA
14
OLDHAM MARKET PLACE
NBU 505

CHAPEL ROAD
A
NBU 511

Oldham's last new rear platform double-deckers arrived in 1958 and 1959 and would sweep away the last remaining pre-war buses in the fleet. They were 44 Leyland PD2/30s with bodies by Metro-Cammell, Roe and Northern Counties. Metro-Cammell-bodied number 422 (PBU 922) has just passed under Mumps Bridge on its way from Denshaw to Chadderton Hall Park. ***(MMT)***

Another Metro-Cammell-bodied example, number 427 (PBU 927) is pictured before delivery. ***(MMT)***

Roe-bodied number 431 (PBU 931) is photographed on its way to Waterhead on service 98. ***(MMT)***

A Northern Counties example, number 460 (PBU 960), stands on Rochdale Corporation's Smith Street Bus Park between journeys on service 24. ***(MMT)***

9 – *THE SWINGING SIXTIES*

A new look

Most people will remember the 1960s as the swinging sixties; a time when Britain finally broke away from the shackles of rationing and controls. It was an exciting time with new fashions, new designs and new freedoms, but it was also a period when wage inflation started to soar and the viability of the bus industry began to deteriorate. The vicious downward spiral of rising costs, fare increases and loss of passengers, followed by further fare increases, gathered momentum. Services were pruned back but fixed costs remained substantially the same and more income had to be raised from fewer and fewer passengers. Against this background momentous changes would occur which would bring about the end of Oldham Corporation Transport's independent existence.

Cyril Page, who had been Oldham's General Manager since March 1944 and who had overseen the rebuilding of bus operations during the difficult post-war years, retired at the end of September 1961 and was succeeded by Harry Taylor who had come from Liverpool to become deputy General Manager two years previously. Mr Taylor would be Oldham's last General Manager and would later become Chief Engineer of SELNEC PTE's Central Division.

In November 1961 The Transport Committee agreed to a proposal by Mr Taylor to change their bus purchasing policy from the then current practice of buying buses in large quantities at lengthy intervals to smaller numbers on an annual basis, the advantages being a smoothing out of the peaks and troughs in the workload and also spreading the costs. The Committee agreed to an initial purchase of 39 buses over a three year period and it was decided to test the market by borrowing three examples of different types for evaluation.

The maximum permitted length for two-axle double-deckers had been increased to 30ft since 1st July 1956 and all of the borrowed buses were built to that length. So far most manufacturers had simply lengthened their existing models but Oldham had stuck to the shorter version. However, the rear-engined Leyland Atlantean was now in production and neighbouring Manchester, after a lengthy battle with the trade unions, had ten examples in operation. So Manchester's Metro-Cammell-bodied 3621, the first of the batch, was borrowed during July 1962, together with Halifax 206, a conventional Leyland Titan PD3/4 with a Metro-Cammell 72-seat front-entrance body, exposed radiator and syncromesh gearbox and Huddersfield 406, a slightly more exotic Leyland Titan PD3A/2 with a front-entrance 70-seat body by Roe sporting a new-style glass-fibre bonnet and pneumocyclic gearbox.

After inspecting all three models, the Committee agreed in principle to buy twenty six 30ft long double-deckers in two equal batches to be delivered in 1964 and 1965 respectively. However, the remaining Crossley single-deckers were now fifteen years old and were feeling their age, so two more buses were borrowed in 1963. One was Manchester's Park Royal-bodied Leyland Tiger Cub number 59, a two door model with 38 semi-coach seats. Painted in the airport service livery of two-tone blue and silver it was designed for one-man operation, Manchester using it on short routes in the suburbs and on airport and trooping contracts. The second bus was L623, a Liverpool Atlantean carrying a Metro-Cammell body of a more pleasing design than the standard one fitted to the Manchester example. Among other things it featured a peaked front to the upper deck which was to become a feature of all Oldham's Atlanteans.

So, the orders were subsequently amended to ten double-deck and six single-deck buses in the first year and ten more double-deckers in the second year. The chassis orders once again went to Leyland, a mixture of ten 73-seat Roe-bodied Titan PD3/5s, ten 77-seat Atlantean PDR1/2s, four bodied by East Lancashire Coachbuilders of Blackburn, a builder new to Oldham and six by Roe and six Tiger Cubs with 41-seat two-door bodies. It was originally intended to award the contract for the single-deckers to Marshall of Cambridge, but after some acrimonious discussion this was reduced to four, the remaining two being built by local firm Pennine Coachcraft. Mr Taylor stamped his own identity on the vehicles with a new look front indicator layout, having destination, intermediate and three-track service number blinds all contained in a single large aperture which was to become standard for all future deliveries. In addition a new fleet numbering series was introduced starting

In order to test the market for 30ft buses Harry Taylor borrowed three examples from other operators during 1962, the one which most impressed being Huddersfield Corporation Roe-bodied Leyland PD3A/2 number 406 pictured above. ***(JJH)***

The resulting order was for similar Leyland PD3/5s of which ten arrived in 1964. Number 109 (109 HBU) is pictured when new outside the gates to Alexandra Park, a favourite spot for photographing new buses. ***(STA)***

Two more buses were borrowed the following year. Manchester's 59 was a Leyland Tiger Cub with a Park Royal two-door body designed for one-man operation. In the upper picture it stands at the Bar Gap Road terminus of service C before leaving for Middleton Junction. ***(JJH)***

Following the visit of Manchester 59 the current orders were modified to include six Tiger Cubs with Marshall bodies. However, they were further changed and the last two were bodied instead by Pennine Coachcraft, a subsidiary of local chassis-builder Seddon. Marshall-bodied number 113 (113 JBU) is shown above at Alexandra Park while number 115 (115 JBU) stands outside the Seddon factory. ***(both STA)***

By contrast the other bus was Liverpool Leyland Atlantean L623 with an upgraded version of the Metro-Cammell body seen at the Gardeners Arms, Moston terminus of service D. ***(STA)***

The last ten buses arrived as Leyland Atlantean PDR1/2s with a Roe 77-seat body sporting a Liverpool-style peak to the front of the upper deck and were the last to be painted new in the traditional crimson lake livery. Number 129 (CBU 129C) became SELNEC 5129 and was withdrawn in 1978, passing to Cherry of Beverley, East Yorkshire. ***(STA)***

With a shortage of single-deckers and a long wait for replacements, Crossley 299 (DBU 299) dating from 1948 was refurbished and fitted with a second-hand Crossley body during 1965. 299 stands in the yard at Wallshaw Street soon after returning to service. It lasted another three years before being withdrawn in 1968. ***(JJH)***

at 101 with the PD3s and painted fleet numbers would also be replaced by cast metal plates. But more changes were to come as Mr Taylor set out to change the fleet's dated image to something more modern and vibrant in tune with the new decade.

The first of the new buses were the PD3s 101-10, number 103 arriving in April 1964. It got a mixed reception, not all passengers appreciating the platform doors which, while keeping the interior warm and helping to reduce accidents, slowed the service down and prevented them jumping on and off between stops. The O.600 engine that had powered all Oldham's smaller PD2s since 1947, performed well enough on the level but drivers complained that the buses were underpowered on hilly routes. Number 108 was scrapped after being damaged beyond repair in an accident at the junction of West Street and King Street in November 1967.

The six single-deckers 111-6 arrived during the next few months and enabled some of the ailing Crossleys to be withdrawn. An attempt was made to obtain some second-hand single-deckers to replace the rest but nothing suitable was available so they would just have to struggle on and another four Tiger Cubs were ordered, again with Marshall bodies. These would not arrive until 1967 and by then the order would have been changed to the rear-engined Panther Cub, but the numbers 117-20 were reserved for them. However, a similar Crossley with a damaged chassis was bought from Southport Corporation and its body, which was in good condition, was transferred to Oldham 299 in the Wallshaw Street body shop during 1965.

The ten Atlanteans, now numbered 121-30, arrived in the summer of 1965. East Lancs had been unable to meet Oldham's delivery deadline so the contract had been taken over by Roe. The bodies were of a much more pleasing design than some on Atlantean chassis and the Liverpool influence was obvious in the detail.

Oldham's Crimson Lake and White livery and its pattern of application had not changed significantly since it was first applied to the tram fleet in 1901 and, coupled with the ageing rear platform body design, was looking decidedly old fashioned although few of the town's citizens would have agreed. Imagine the reaction then when, in late 1963, Leyland PD2 number 402 emerged from the Wallshaw Street paint shop in a striking two-tone blue livery obviously inspired by Manchester's number 59. This did not go down well with the public who considered it garish and undignified and the experiment was not repeated although 402 remained blue for a few years.

However, in 1966 Mr Taylor tried again, this time with a less revolutionary and therefore more acceptable combination of Pommard, and Devon Cream which would become the new standard livery. Atlantean 130 was the last new bus to be delivered in Crimson Lake. The next batch of new buses already on order would come in Pommard.

More changes

More changes were made to the route network in the next few years, mainly due to the continued expansion of the Holts and Limeside estates and the building of the new Alt estate to the south of Abbey Hills Road. First, in July 1962, services 4 and V (Town Hall-Holts) were diverted in and out of Alt estate. Again, this was only a temporary expedient and on 22nd September 1963 a more comprehensive scheme was implemented which involved swapping the legs of several cross-town routes to balance loadings and to make economies.

To cater for the Limeside estate, service A (Greenacres-Chapel Road) was extended further along Chapel Road along the 7 route with alternate journeys diverted via Heron Street using the vacant letter H and providing a circular route through Limeside. Service 7 (Limeside-Higginshaw) was reduced to peak period operation and diverted to Bar Gap Road and service C was then taken off Bar Gap Road and sent to Higginshaw along Egerton Street and the line of the long-withdrawn tram route. Service 4 no longer ran via Alt Estate, which was then served by G between Oldham and Alt via Waterloo Street.

Two other minor changes were introduced at the same time; service B was extended a short distance within the Fitton Hill estate and services 5 and 6 were extended from Burnley Lane to Chadderton Hall Park.

Meanwhile, on 5th July Manchester's service 82 between Chorlton and Hollinwood had been extended through to Waterhead, replacing alternate journeys on 98 and achieving considerable economies between Manchester and Hollinwood. To avoid costly route learning Oldham's share of the timetable was restricted to the 98 while Manchester worked all of the 82 journeys.

With five narrow streets feeding into it, the roundabout at the Market Place was becoming a major source of traffic congestion by the mid-sixties. So, on 26th March 1965 the upper part of Manchester Street was closed to through traffic and a gyratory scheme was introduced involving George Street, Barn Street, King Street, St Domingo Street, Duke Street and West Street involving the majority of Oldham's bus routes and incidentally ending the historic route of service 34 which had been the only service to operate along Crossbank Street since its inception as the Oldham to Northenden express service in 1930. A slight modification in December 1966 closed Duke Street and re-routed buses through a new cut-through from St Domingo Street into West Street. The routes would then remain unchanged until a succession of major developments of the town centre in PTE days.

Oldham in crisis

Having temporarily dealt with the relatively minor crisis of the Crossley single-deckers, Oldham now found itself faced with another one of major proportions. In October 1965 a spot check by Ministry of Transport vehicle examiners resulted in stop orders being put on a total of 97 buses, nearly half the fleet. Mostly these were for bodywork defects; nearly half were relatively minor and were rectified within the next few days, but eight were so bad that the buses were immediately withdrawn from service as being beyond economic repair. Neighbouring operators rallied round and a total of 45 buses were drafted in from around the area in order to maintain services. The buses involved were mostly older vehicles, the only exceptions being from Bradford and Stockport, and were generally used on peak hour duties.

An investigation into the causes of the problems, put before the full Council on 2nd February 1966, concluded that for many years too little provision had been made for the maintenance of an ageing fleet. Mr Taylor had begun to address this by introducing a planned fleet replacement programme but this would take time to work through and meanwhile sufficient second hand buses should be purchased. In all twelve buses had already been acquired, all Leyland PD2s with Leyland bodies and in the end just four more would be needed. The buses involved took fleet numbers carrying on from the last Oldham PD2s. They were:

463-466	Sheffield	1949
467-470	Halifax	1947/48
471-474	Bolton	1949
475-478	Sheffield	1952

BUSES HIRED 1965

Operator	Fleet Nos.	Reg. Nos.	Chassis	Body	New
Bolton	400 401/26/7/34/8	CWH 750 DBN 304/29/ 30/7/41	Leyland PD2/4	Leyland H58R	1949
Bradford	207-9	6207-9 KW	AEC Regent V	MCCW H70F	1964
Bury	158/9	EN 9958/9	Leyland PD2/3	Weymann H56R	1949
Manchester	3175/6/9 3266/7/70/ 6/7/80/1	JNA 476/7/500 JND 667/8/71/ 7/8/81/2	Leyland PD1/3 Leyland PD2/6	MCCW H58R Leyland H58R	1949/50 1950
Rochdale	227-9/33	HDK 27-9/833	AEC Regent III	Weymann	1949/51
St Helens	E74/6/80	CDJ 719/21/880	Leyland PD2/10	Davies H56R	1954
Salford	407-12	CRJ 407-12	Daimler CVG6	MCCW H54R	1950
Stockport	24/5	BJA 924/5	Leyland PD2/40	E Lancs H64R	1964
Wigan	25/7 32, 163	JP 6018/28 JP 8317/26	Leyland PD1 Leyland PD2/1	Leyland L53R Leyland H56R	1947 1950

A Rochdale cream and blue Weymann-bodied AEC Regent III, a maroon Bolton all-Leyland PD2/4 and the two light green Weymann-bodied Leyland PD1/3s from Bury add a splash of colour to Wallshaw Street depot in October 1965. ***(STA)***

All were painted in Oldham livery before delivery, 463-74 in crimson lake and 475-8 in Pommard. They served Oldham well, all but the Halifax vehicles lasting into SELNEC days. Number 471 (SELNEC 5371) is preserved at the Bolton Transport Museum.

Luckily, the next order for new buses, 17 Atlanteans numbered 131-47, started to arrive early in 1966 and took some of the pressure off. The first five vehicles were bodied by East Lancs and the remaining twelve by Roe and only differed from the previous ten in minor details, perhaps the most noticeable being the full length translucent roof panel on the upper deck. Number 146, the first of the Roe-bodied buses, was displayed on that body builder's stand at the Commercial Motor Show and later outside the Town Hall with its tyres painted white for the occasion. Together with the 16 second hand buses they enabled many of the older and more problematical vehicles to be withdrawn, including all the remaining Daimlers as well as a number of the PD1s dating from 1946/47.

The 1967 deliveries comprised a further 17 buses. Thirteen of these, 148-60, were more Atlanteans, the first five bodies again being allocated to East Lancs, who sub-contracted them to their Neepsend subsidiary in Sheffield , and the remainder to Roe. The last four were 117-20, the four Marshall-bodied Leyland Panther Cubs that saw the final demise of most of the single-deck Crossleys, the one exception being 299 which had been fitted with the Southport body in 1965. The other remaining Crossley was 368 of the 1950 quartet of double-deckers which would later be preserved. Apart from this Oldham was now left with a wholly Leyland fleet.

One-man operation

Arguably the greatest potential for economy was one-man operation. Oldham had tried it on the Coppice route in 1924 but had given it up by 1926. Then, on 1st July 1966, after a great deal of pressure from the bus operators, the Government finally authorised one-man operation of double-deck buses. However, the first conversion of the modern era came on 29th August 1966 when single-deck service F (Royton-Shore Edge) was converted using one of the Tiger Cubs. At the same time the service was numbered 17 which was the first step in changing from a mix of letters and numbers to a full numeric system using the

Following the problems of 1965, 12 second-hand vehicles were acquired to bridge the gap before the arrival of new buses. Four came from each of Halifax, Bolton and Sheffield, all Leyland PD2s of various types. A further four arrived from Sheffield the following year. Most lasted long enough to pass into SELNEC ownership. The upper photograph shows number 469 (ACP 388), a Halifax PD2/1 seen on Ashton Road on its way to depot after working a peak period journey to Hathershaw. A Vauxhall Victor passes in the opposite direction while a Wolseley car and an Ashton Corporation Leyland on service 9 follow behind. ***(STA)***

In the middle picture number 474 (DBN 341), a former Bolton PD2/4, stands at the Wren's Nest terminus ready to leave on a service 3 journey to Mills Hill while at the bottom former Sheffield PD2/10 number 475 (OWB 856) turns round at Bar Gap Road. ***(both JJH)***

The first of the 1966 delivery of Leyland Atlanteans and the first bus to delivered in the new Pommard livery was number 131 (EBU 131G) with body by East Lancashire Coachbuilders. It is seen passing the Town Hall on High Street on its way to Manchester on service 98. ***(STA)***

In 1967 Oldham took delivery of four Leyland Panther Cubs with Marshall bodies. Number 119 (LBU 119E) stands outside the Marshall factory at Cambridge. ***(STA)***

Oldham liked to line up its new buses in numerical order for publicity purposes. Here numbers 153-9 (LBU 153-9E) act as a backdrop to their official handover to the Mayor of Oldham in 1967. ***(STA)***

Six Marshall-bodied Leyland Panthers also arrived during 1968 to extend one-man operation. Number 172 (OBU 172F) seen here working a private hire duty became 5022 in the PTE fleet, but had a short life in Oldham. Together with other non-standard SELNEC single-deckers it emigrated to Australia where it joined the fleet of Keiraville Bus Services of Fairy Meadow, New South Wales. ***(JJH)***

newer buses which were equipped with the three-track number blinds. With the introduction of the Panther Cubs it was possible to convert more services and C (Higginshaw-Middleton Junction) and E (Town Hall-Upper Mossley) became driver-only operated later in the year and renumbered 15 and 16 respectively, 16 being the number already shown by the SHMD buses on the Mossley service. Electrically driven TIM ticket issuing machines were used mounted on the cab side ahead of the driver.

At this time Oldham's policy was to use single-deck one-man buses on lighter loaded services, while retaining double-deck crew operation on the more heavily patronised trunk routes. In order to achieve savings at peak periods all future double-deck orders were to be high capacity rear-engined vehicles which would also be suitable for one-man operation and therefore eligible for Government grants of up to 50%. However, this would take some time to achieve as it was too late to modify the order for 161-71, the next batch of eleven Roe-bodied Atlanteans which were shortly to be delivered.

On 1st April 1968 all the remaining lettered services were given numbers, bringing to an end the alphabetic system which had started with the introduction of the Chadderton-New Moston service in 1925 and marking what would be the final act in modernising the Department's image. The full list of services at that date was:

1	Waterhead-Hollinwood
2	Newhey-Manchester
3	Rushcroft-Mills Hill
4	Chadderton-Sholver/Denshaw
5	Chadderton-Denshaw
6	Chadderton-Strinesdale
7	Limeside-Higginshaw
8	Shaw-Hollinwood (20)
9	Rochdale-Ashton
10	Greenfield-Manchester
11	Derker-Stottfield
12	Derker-Middleton
13	Uppermill-Manchester
14	Uppermill-Manchester
15	Higginshaw-Middleton Junction (C)
16	Oldham-Upper Mossley (E)
17	Royton-Shore Edge (F)
18	Limeside-Chapel Road-Greenacres (A)
19	Limeside-Heron St-Greenacres (H)
20	Shaw-Hollinwood (8)
21	Fitton Hill-Middleton Junction (B)
22	Rhodes Bank-Moston (D)
23	Oldham-Alt Estate (G)
24	Rochdale-Royton-Manchester
25	Oldham-Holts (4)
26	Oldham-Holts (V)
27	Hollinwood-Grotton (T)
28	Hollinwood-Lees (O)
29	Hollinwood-Stamford Road (O)
56	Hollinwood-Cheetham Hill
59	Shaw-Middleton-Manchester
82	Waterhead-Manchester-Chorlton
90	Rochdale-Manchester express
98	Waterhead-Manchester
134	Oldham-Manchester express
153	Oldham-Uppermill circular
155	Oldham-Uppermill circular

Six Marshall-bodied Leyland Panthers, a longer and more powerful version of the Panther Cub with the large O.680 engine, also arrived in 1968. These were put to work on services 22 and 153/155, initially crew operated, until they were converted to OMO on 29th December.

Eleven more Leyland Atlanteans were delivered in 1968, one of which number 167 (OBU 167F) is pictured travelling along Mumps on service 26. As a circular through the town centre buses showed "HOLTS ESTATE" throughout the route. ***(MMT)***

Atlantean number 181 (SBU 181G) was the penultimate bus delivered to Oldham Corporation before its absorption into SELNEC. The Roe body was extensively modified for one-man operation, noticeable changes being the centre exit door and the repositioned indicator enabling the driver to change the blinds without leaving the cab. The coin-in-the-slot symbols on the front between decks were supposed to tell passengers that the bus was fitted with a farebox. ***(STA)***

For some time it had been intended to run a service to Sholver, another windswept council estate on the moors between Moorside and Grains Bar by utilising journeys on services 5 and 6. The vacant number 4 was allocated but the service did not start until 15th January 1969, once again due to the lack of a suitable access road.

Oldham's final deliveries were 178-82, five Atlanteans with longer two-door Roe bodies designed for one-man operation with a forward ascending staircase opposite the centre exit door. The redesigned cab incorporated a right hand gear change to keep it clear of the ticket machine, the front indicator box was lowered to a position just above the front windscreen so that the driver could change it without leaving his seat, and a periscope gave a view of the upper deck. They entered service in April 1969, working on services 25 and 26 to Holts, driver-only operated from 8th June. Fare collection was initially by an American designed Johnson fare-box, with no tickets being issued and no change given, but these were later replaced by a simpler box of the pattern used at Bolton and known as 'Bolton boxes'. The system was wide open to abuse, but was retained until the PTE implemented a common policy across the whole network.

The 1968 Transport Act

There had already been three abortive attempts to introduce differing degrees of co-ordination and integration of bus services in the Manchester conurbation; the Joint Committee of the twenties, the SELNEC scheme of the thirties and the Area Transport Boards in the forties, but these had all fallen by the wayside. However, with the rapid decline in traffic and with costs and fares soaring something had to be done before public transport in Britain followed that of America into near oblivion.

During 1962 the Transport Users Consultative Committee was becoming concerned about the position and wrote to Oldham suggesting that '*a full enquiry into the needs of the passenger suburban road and rail services of the Manchester conurbation and South East Lancashire and North East Cheshire generally should be made as a matter of urgency, and that the local authorities and independent bus undertakings in the area should take the initiative and jointly organise a comprehensive survey of all their traffic problems.*' Subsequently, in June 1963 a meeting of the interested parties was held in Manchester, but nothing came of it and the following year a left wing Labour Government came to power, committed to an integrated transport system.

Aware that total nationalisation was no longer a serious political option, attention was focused on the major conurbations and in 1965 the then Minister of Transport, Mrs Barbara Castle, produced a White Paper called 'Transport Policy' proposing the creation of a number of Conurbation Transport Authorities to plan, manage and finance the operation of local transport within their areas. They would also be responsible for land use and highway planning and even car parking policy. The one which included Oldham bore the ponderous title of 'South East Lancashire and North East Cheshire', which was abbreviated to SELNEC and centered on Manchester. Initially, a small group was set up to look at transport problems in the area and to identify possible solutions. Known as the SELNEC Area Land Use and Transportation Study or SALTS for short, it was largely funded by the Government with contributions from the constituent local authorities.

While Oldham, like most other local authorities, accepted the need for some form of integration, and indeed amalgamation, they were unhappy about an outside body being able to set service levels and fares without consultation, exactly the same reason that the SELNEC scheme had foundered some thirty years earlier.

After lengthy consultation a further White Paper, 'Public Transport and Planning', was produced in 1967. This proposed a two-tier organisation with a Passenger Transport Authority, consisting of elected members of the constituent authorities, to set policy and a professional Passenger Transport Executive to carry it out. The Executive would acquire the assets of the local authorities and would operate the services. The White Paper became the 1968 Transport Act, which came into force on 1st April 1969, a date that its critics deemed appropriate, and the Passenger Transport Authority took over.

For a time, while the PTA formulated its strategy, the Council continued to be responsible for day to day operation until the Passenger Transport Executive was formed. The Executive came into being on 1st November 1969 and Oldham Corporation Transport Department ceased to exist.

10 – LIFE AFTER OLDHAM

Into SELNEC

Things did not change overnight. The PTE organised the eleven former municipal bus undertakings into three divisions, Northern, Central and Southern, Oldham becoming a District of the Southern Division, which had its headquarters in the former Stockport Corporation Transport head office at Daw Bank. In addition to Oldham and Stockport it also included Ashton and the SHMD Joint Board. Oldham contributed a total of 185 buses to the new organisation, all of Leyland manufacture but with a mixture of bodies from nine different builders, Crossley, East Lancs, Leyland, Marshall, Metro-Cammell, Neepsend, Northern Counties, Pennine and of course Roe.

The first outward sign of things to come was the new Sunglow Orange and White livery which started to appear on the buses in the following March. At the same time SELNEC's new logo, a stylised 'S' together with the divisional name, was applied to all buses, whether repainted or not and, more controversially, the existing municipal coats of arms were removed from the vehicle sides. Oldham's buses gained a green 'lazy S' with the name 'Southern' in black. The next step was to introduce a unified fleet numbering scheme, Southern Division buses being renumbered between 5000 and 5999. Oldham's single-deckers were numbered between 5011 and 5027 and the double-deckers between 5101 and 5378. The new numbers were applied haphazardly and in different styles of lettering dependant upon what was available at the time, although it all got sorted out eventually with black numerals being applied on repainting. One oddity was Atlantean 171, the first Oldham bus to repainted, which was turned out in orange and white with the SELNEC Southern logo and its Oldham fleet number for a press launch of the new livery on Manchester's rain-swept training yard at Ardwick.

Buses which the Corporation had ordered during the last years of the Department's existence were delivered to SELNEC and initially went to Oldham and were given the numbers they would have received had they originally gone to the Corporation. First in 1970 came five Roe-bodied Atlanteans following on from the 178-82 batch, numbered 5183-7 and painted in Oldham Pommard. Then in 1971 came a further twelve numbered 5188-99 and painted in SELNEC orange. All outstanding orders were now delivered and there was a pause while various options were considered.

A start was made on withdrawing the oldest buses and by the end of 1970 20 vehicles had gone, one (246) dating from 1947! 246 was saved for preservation and is now on display at the Museum of Transport in Manchester. To balance withdrawals and new deliveries and to speed up the conversion to one man operation, transfers of buses within and between the divisions were common. In the early days there was inevitably some confusion about autonomy and ad-hoc decisions led to some oddities. Stockport's all-Leyland PD2 302 went to Oldham and was quickly painted in the Pommard livery and given fleet number 5202 in the Oldham block but was soon renumbered to 5922 in the Stockport series, to which it had been allocated officially. Oldham Atlanteans 5127 and 5138 went in the opposite direction. In another notable move six Manchester two-door Leyland Tiger Cubs, 10-15, came to Oldham for one-man routes still in their red livery and were renumbered 5000-5. By one of those strange quirks of fate 5004 had originally been Manchester 59, borrowed for evaluation in 1963 and whose then two-tone blue livery had inspired Harry Taylor's experiment with 402.

Meanwhile, behind the scenes a lot of work was being carried out into standardisation of wages, conditions and operating practices, most of which went un-noticed by the general public, although a necessary but unfortunately timed 15% increase in fares did not. More obvious was the comprehensive service-numbering scheme. For a time services continued to show the numbers used by their former operators and it was not until 1972 that SELNEC developed a single unified scheme. Renumbering was implemented in stages over several months starting in November 1972 and Oldham services were renumbered in December 1973, mostly by having 400 added.

One of SELNEC's responsibilities was to co-ordinate services within its area. The North Western Road Car Company, with whom Oldham had had a joint operating agreement since 1927, was based in Stockport and 60% of its mileage was run within the conurbation. So the PTE

The first outward sign of the new regime was the appearance of orange buses on the streets of Oldham. Marshall-bodied Leyland Tiger Cub number 114 (114 JBU), now SELNEC 5014, displays its new colours including the green Southern flash, at Alexandra Park when fresh out of the Wallshaw Street paint shop. ***(JJH)***

17 Roe-bodied Leyland Atlanteans were delivered to Oldham after the takeover date. Number 5198 (ABU 198J), numerically the penultimate Oldham bus, arrived in 1971 in full SELNEC orange livery. It is seen here posed outside the depot on arrival. ***(JJH)***

To speed up conversions to one-man operation across the area buses were transferred between depots. Ashton was one place with a lower than average proportion of OMO and suitable buses were moved there. Oldham's number 5183 (WBU 183H), which had been delivered in 1970 in Pommard livery, was one of these and stands in Ashton Bus Station while working the newly converted Hurst Circular service. ***(MMT)***

However, there were moves the other way, one of which in 1974 resulted in a number of Rochdale's rear platform AEC Regent Vs moving to Oldham, the first vehicles of this make to run there since the sole batch of eight AEC 507 open-top double-deckers between 1925 and 1934. Two of these stand in the depot waiting to go out on evening peak duties. ***(MMT)***

purchased that part of the company and ran it for a time as a separate wholly-owned subsidiary called SELNEC Cheshire with its own brown 'lazy S' logo and the fleet name 'Cheshire' in black. Buses retained their existing North Western fleet numbers and were gradually painted into orange and white. SELNEC Cheshire was wound up on 21st May 1973, its Oldham depot in Clegg Street was closed and its operations in the Saddleworth and Crompton areas, together with 30 buses and all the staff, were transferred en bloc to Wallshaw Street and integrated with the former Corporation routes. North Western services taken over by Oldham at that time were:

2	Newhey-Manchester
10	Greenfield-Manchester
13/14	Uppermill-Manchester
153/155	Uppermill-Oldham circular
157	Diggle-Uppermill-Mossley
158	Denshaw-Uppermill-Mossley
159	Woodhouses-Middleton

2, 10, 13, 14, 153 and 155 were already jointly operated with Oldham.

As one-man operation increased and new standard buses were delivered, more and more older vehicles were moved around. In one of the more interesting transfers six former Rochdale half-cab AEC Regent Vs came to Oldham. But now as 1973 moved into 1974 more important changes were in the pipeline.

Greater Manchester

As a result of the 1973 Local Government Act the SELNEC Passenger Transport Authority was abolished and overall transport strategy came directly under the control of the newly formed Greater Manchester Council from 1st April 1974. The bus and rail operations became the Greater Manchester PTE with a new 'wiggly M' logo and the title 'Greater Manchester Transport'.

Outwardly, however, this was the only change. The last rear platform half-cab double-decker 436, by now numbered 5336, a Roe-bodied Leyland Titan PD2/30, went in 1977 and the last former Oldham bus 5194, a Leyland Atlantean delivered to SELNEC in 1971, drew the final curtain in 1983. In 1981 GMT introduced a new livery retaining orange as the main body colour but with a white roof and upper deck window surrounds and a brown skirt. Atlantean 5188 gained a brief moment of fame as the only former Oldham bus to carry the new livery when it was mistakenly painted in the new colour scheme, the bus which should have been painted being standard Fleetline number 7188.

Further re-organisation of the management structure in 1981 created four areas, North, South, East and West, Oldham becoming part of the new East area along with Stockport, Tameside, Glossop and the two former Manchester depots at Birchfields Road and Hyde Road and, together with the other districts, was reduced to depot status, decision-making being concentrated in the new East Division headquarters at Wallshaw Street.

The present day

The only remaining trace of Oldham Corporation's once proud Transport Department, which had provided tram and bus services in the Borough and surrounding districts for 66 years, is the former depot and offices at Wallshaw Street, now the headquarters of First Group company, First Manchester. Since the break up and subsequent privatisation of Greater Manchester Buses, First Manchester runs most of the local services while Stagecoach Manchester also runs into the town, mostly from the south on services operating from Hyde Road. A number of small operators can also be seen, but the crimson lake and white half cab double-decker, with its open platform Roe body once so synonymous with municipal transport in Oldham is now just a memory.

In 1972 SELNEC took delivery of eight 11.3 metre Leyland Nationals with two-door bodies and numbered them in the experimental fleet and carried an orange SELNEC flash. EX33 (TXJ 510K) was originally allocated to Bolton but later came to Oldham a couple of years later where it is seen leaving the garage suitably decorated to take part in a carnival procession. ***(JJH)***

During 1993 SELNEC's successor Greater Manchester Buses was split into two semi-autonomous divisions known as GMBuses North and GMBuses South prior to being sold to an employees' buy out on 31st March 1994. Oldham was included in the Northern company which would eventually become First Manchester. The picture shows MCW Metrobus number 5069 (MRJ 69W) working on service 409 between Rochdale and Ashton in the short-lived orange, white and black livery of GMBuses North. ***(MMT)***

SELNEC SERVICE RENUMBERING 1974

SELNEC No.	Route	Oldham No.
23	Rochdale-Royton-Manchester express	90
24	Rochdale-Royton-Chadderton-Manchester	24
59	Shaw-Heyside-Oldham-Chadderton-Middleton-Manchester	59
82	Waterhead-Oldham-Hollinwood-Manchester-Chorlton	82
98	Waterhead-Oldham-Hollinwood-Manchester	98
134	Oldham-Hollinwood-Manchester express	134
147	Hollinwood-Moston-Manchester	147
159	Woodhouses-Moston-Middleton	159
180	Greenfield-Oldham-Hollinwood-Manchester express	10
181	Newhey-Heyside-Royton-Chadderton-Manchester	2
182	Newhey-Cowlishaw-Royton-Chadderton-Manchester	2
183	Uppermill-Waterhead-Oldham-Hollinwood-Manchester express	13
184	Uppermill-Lees-Oldham-Hollinwood-Manchester express	14
403	Rushcroft-Shaw-Cowlishaw-Oldham-Chadderton-Mills Hill-Middleton	3
404	Sholver-Moorside-Oldham-Hollinwood	4
405	Denshaw-Grains Bar-Moorside-Oldham-Hollinwood	5
406	Strinesdale-Moorside-Oldham-Hollinwood	6
407	Bar Gap Road-Oldham-Chapel Road-Limeside	7
408	Oldham-Hurst Cross-Stalybridge	8
409	Rochdale-Royton-Oldham-Hathershaw-Ashton	9
410	Summit-Royton-Oldham-Hathershaw	34
411	Derker-Oldham-Royton-Stottfield	11
412	Derker-Oldham-Royton-Mills Hill-Middleton	12
415	Higginshaw-Oldham-Chadderton-Middleton Junction-Mainway	15
416	Oldham-Lees-Mossley	16
417	Royton-High Crompton-Shaw-Shore Edge	17
418	Greenacres-Oldham-Chapel Road-Limeside	18
419	Greenacres-Oldham-Heron Street-Limeside	19
420	Shaw-Cowlishaw-Royton-Werneth-Hollinwood	20
421	Fitton Hill-Oldham-Chadderton	21
422	Oldham-Werneth-Butler Green-Moston	22
423	Oldham-Alt	23
425	Oldham-Glodwick circular-Holts	25
426	Oldham-Glodwick circular-Holts	26
427	Grotton-Lees-Oldham-Hollinwood	27
429	Stamford Road-Lees-Oldham-Hollinwood	29
433	Oldham-Waterhead-Uppermill-Lees-Oldham circular	153
435	Oldham-Lees-Uppermill-Waterhead-Oldham circular	155
437	Diggle-Uppermill-Mossley	157
438	Denshaw-Delph-Uppermill-Mossley	158

APPENDIX 2 – BUS AND TROLLEYBUS FLEET LIST

Year	Reg. Nos.	Fleet Nos.	Chassis	Body	Notes
1913	BU401-3	-	Tilling-Stevens TTA2	Tilling-Stevens O34RO	1
1918	BU69	-	Electromobile	Tilling Stevens O34RO	2
1924	BU3402-6	1-5	Leyland C9	Leyland B24F	
1925	BU3672-5	6-9	Leyland C7	Leyland B28F	
1925	TB2553	10	Leyland	?	3
1925	BU3861/54	1/2	Railless Trolleybus	Short Bros B36C	
1926	BU3991-8	10-7	AEC507	Roe H52RO	
1926	BU4509-11	18-20	Guy BX	Roe H60RO	
1926/7	BU4574-80	21-7	Guy BKX	Guy B32R	
1927	BU4838/9	28/9	Karrier WL6/1	Short Bros B39R	
1927	BU4840-2	30-2	Guy FCX	Roe B39R	
1927	BU4843/4	33/4	Guy FCX	Roe H56RO	
1928	BU5172	35	Karrier DD6/1	Hall Lewis H70R	
1928	BU5173	36	Guy FCX	Short Bros H72R	
1928	BU5264/2/7/3/6/5	37-42	Karrier CL6	Hall Lewis B33R	
1928	BU5550-5	43-8	Karrier DD6	English Electric H66R	
1928	BU5556-63	49-56	Guy FCX	English Electriv H66R	
1929	WH1352	57	ADC426	Bell B32D	4
1929	WH1441	58	ADC426	Burlingham B32D	4
1931	BU6760-3	59-62	Leyland Tiger TS3	Roe B31F	
1932	BU7102-5	63-6	Leyland Tiger TS4	Roe B33F	
1932	BU7106	67	Leyland Tiger TS4	Shearing & Crabtree B31F	
1932	BU7107-14	68-75	Leyland Titan TD2	Leyland H51R	
1933	BU7600-7	10-17	Leyland Titan TD2	English Electric H54R	
1933	BU7608-16	21-9	Leyland Tiger TS4	Roe B32F	
1934	BU7945	57	Crossley Mancunian	Roe H53R	
1934	BU7946	58	Leyland Titan TD3	English Electric H54R	
1934	BU8254-6	18-20	Leyland Tiger TS6	Roe FB32F	
1934	BU8257-62	30-5	Leyland Titan TD3	Roe H54R	
1935	BU8421-5	1-5	Crossley Mancunian	Roe H53R	
1935	BU8426-51	76-101	Leyland Titan TD3	Roe H54R	
1935	BU8573-5	102-4	Leyland Titan TD4	Leyland H52R	
1936	BU8860	105	Leyland Titan TD4	Metro-Cammell H56R	
1935	BU8861-4	106-9	Leyland Titan TD4	English Electric H56R	
1935	BU8865-8	110-3	Leyland Titan TD4	Roe H56R	
1935/6	BU8972-4	114-6	Leyland Titan TD4	Roe H56R	
1935	BU8975-7	117-9	Leyland Titan TD4	English Electric H56R	
1936	BU9260-5	36-41	Leyland Titan TD4	English Electric H56R	
1936	BU9266-71	42-7	Leyland Titan TD4	Roe H56R	
1936	BU9621-6	120-5	Leyland Titan TD4	English Electric H56R	
1936	BU9627-32	126-31	Leyland Titan TD4	Roe H56R	
1937	ABU350-70	132-52	Leyland Titan TD5	English Electric H56R	
1937	ABU371-85	153-67	Leyland Titan TD5	Roe H56R	
1937	ABU386-91	168-73	Daimler COG5	Roe H53R	
1938	ABU859-64	174-9	Leyland Titan TD5	Leyland H56R	
1939-41	CBU180-226	180-226	Leyland Titan TD5	Roe H56R	
1944	DDK256	227	Leyland Titan TD5	Leyland H56R	5
1944	DK7378/9	-	Leyland Tiger TS1	Burlingham C29R	6
1946	DBU20-33	228-41	Leyland Titan PD1	Roe H56R	

Year	Reg. Nos.	Fleet Nos.	Chassis	Body	Notes
1947/8	DBU242-91	242-91	Leyland PD1/3	Roe H56R	
1948	DBU292-301	292-301	Crossley SD42/3	Roe B32F	
1948	EBU465-74	302-11	Crossley DD42/4	Crossley H56R	
1948	EBU912-21	312-21	Daimler CVD6	Roe H56R	
1949	EBU922-36	322-36	Daimler CVD6	Crossley H56R	
1948-50	EBU867-81	337-51	Leyland Titan PD2/3	Roe H56R	
1950	FBU639-48	352-61	Leyland Titan PD2/3	Roe H56R	
1950	FBU821-4	362-5	Crossley SD42/7	Roe B32F	
1950	FBU825-8	366-9	Crossley DD42/8	Crossley H56R	
1952	HBU123-5	370-2	Leyland Titan PD2/12	Leyland H56R	
1954/5	KBU373-82	373-82	Leyland Titan PD2/20	Roe H56R	
1955	KBU383-7	383-7	Leyland Titan PD2/20	Metro-Cammell H56R	
1957	NBU488-507	388-407	Leyland Titan PD2/20	Roe H60R	
1957	NBU508-12	408-12	Leyland Titan PD2/20	Crossley H61R	
1957	NBU513-8	413-8	Leyland Titan PD2/20	Northern Counties H61R	
1958/9	PBU919-28	419-28	Leyland Titan PD2/30	Metro-Cammell H65R	
1958	PBU929-52	429-52	Leyland Titan PD2/30	Roe H65R	
1958/9	PBU953-62	453-62	Leyland Titan PD2/30	Northern Counties H65R	
1964	101-10HBU	101-10	Leyland Titan PD3/5	Roe H73F	
1964	111-14JBU	111-4	Leyland Tiger Cub PSUC1/13	Marshall B41D	
1965	115/6JBU	115/6	Leyland Tiger Cub PSUC1/13	Pennine B41D	
1965	CBU121-30C	121-30	Leyland Atlantean PDR1/1	Roe H77F	
1965	LWE104/9-11	463-6	Leyland Titan PD2/1	Leyland H56R	7
1965	ACP 392/85/8/90	467-70	Leyland Titan PD2/1	Leyland H59R	8
1965	DBN329/30/7/42	471-4	Leyland Titan PD2/4	Leyland H58R	9
1966	GBU131-5D	131-5	Leyland Atlantean PDR1/1	East Lancs H77F	
1966	GBU136-47D	136-47	Leyland Atlantean PDR1/1	Roe H77F	
1966	OWB856/7/9/61	475-8	Leyland Titan PD2/10	Leyland H61R	10
1967	LBU148-52E	148-52	Leyland Atlantean PDR1/1	Neepsend H77F	
1967	LBU153-60E	153-60	Leyland Atlantean PDR1/1	Roe H77F	
1967	LBU117-20E	117-20	Leyland Panther Cub PSRC1/1	Marshall B45D	
1967/8	OBU161-71F	161-71	Leyland Atlantean PDR1/1	Roe H77F	
1968	OBU172-7F	172-7	Leyland Panther PSUR1/1	Marshall B48+20D	
1969	SBU178-82G	178-82	Leyland Atlantean PDR1A/1	Roe H74D	
1970	WBU183-7H	183-7	Leyland Atlantean PDR1A/1	Roe H74D	11
1971	ABU188-99J	188-99	Leyland Atlantean PDR1A/1	Roe H74D	11

1 BU403 was originally registered BU11
2 Body from BU401
3 Ex-Belgrave Mills, Oldham
4 Ex-JR Tognarelli, Bolton.New 1928 (57), 1929 (58)
5 Ex-Yelloway.New 1938
6 Ex-Yelloway.New 1931.Not operated by Oldham
7 Ex-Sheffield.New 1949.463 was H59R
8 Ex Halifax.New 1948 (467), others 1947
9 Ex-Bolton.New 1949
10 Ex-Sheffield.New 1952
11 Delivered to SELNEC as 5183-99

GALLERY

EARLY DAYS

Above. A horse tram takes part in a procession down a flag-bedecked High Street. The date is 22nd June 1897, the occasion is Queen Victoria's Diamond Jubilee and the citizens of Oldham are out in force to celebrate. ***(STA)***

Left. Bowler hats and clogs and shawls are well in evidence as passengers queue to board a horse tram on West Street on its journey from Hollinwood to Waterhead at the turn of the century. ***(STA)***

Six years on and the horse trams have gone, replaced by the new electric cars. In this period scene tram number 43 stands in King Street at the Star Inn terminus before leaving for Middleton Road. ***(STA)***

Tram number 31, new in 1902, had already received a top cover when it was photographed some ten years later at Rhodes Bank on its way to Shaw. The tram has just come down Yorkshire Street and Mumps railway bridge can be seen in the background. In this scene, typical of the times, a cart horse labours up the hill in the opposite direction pulling a load of cotton bales. ***(STA)***

Above. On a typically wet day with rain glistening on the cobbles, tram number 17, the first of the 1923 batch, stands on the middle road at Hollinwood waiting to leave for Shaw on service 8. In the background an open balcony car takes the through road on its way from Manchester to Waterhead. Number 17 ran through the war before being withdrawn in 1946. It then passed to the Gateshead and District Tramways where it ran for a further five years. ***(STA)***

Upper left. A busy scene in Manchester's Stevenson Square in 1937. Oldham tram number 4, on service 20 to Waterhead, stands next to a Manchester Corporation lowbridge Crossley. Nine years later number 4 would be the last tram to run in Oldham on the evening of 3rd August 1946. ***(STA)***

Lower left. In this 1937 view at Hollinwood tram number 7 of the second series waits its time before continuing its journey to Manchester while a Manchester Pilcher car has just left in the opposite direction on its way to Waterhead. ***(STA)***

Above. Number 127, one of the final batch of trams dating from 1926, has just arrived at Waterhead, the blind already changed for its return working to Hollinwood. In the background number 7 appears again, ready to leave on service 20 to Manchester. ***(STA)***

Upper right. A typical thirties view of industrial Oldham as 1924 replacement car number 18 pauses to drop passengers at Werneth at the end of its long climb up from Hollinwood. Ahead Manchester Road bears to the right and continues uphill to Oldham, but number 18 will take the left fork down Featherstall Road South on its journey to Shaw. ***(STA)***

Lower right. Winters can be hard in Oldham as shown in this view of a snow-covered Manchester car travelling along High Street on its way to Waterhead. In these conditions Manchester's route number stencils had an advantage over Oldham's roller blinds as the number 20 can still be made out. Note the word OXO scrawled in the snow on the rear headlight. ***(STA)***

Upper. Number 58 (BU 7946) was a diesel-engined Leyland Titan TD4 bought in 1934 to assess its suitability for the coming tramway conversions. It evidently proved satisfactory as many more TD4 and TD5 models were subsequently purchased. It is seen here climbing High Street on its way from Lees to the Market Place on service O. ***(STA)***

Lower. Although this is a main cross-Pennine road, there is a complete lack of traffic at the Junction Inn in Denshaw as number 140 (ABU 358), one of 36 TD5s delivered in 1937, poses for its photograph in the middle of the junction. ***(STA)***

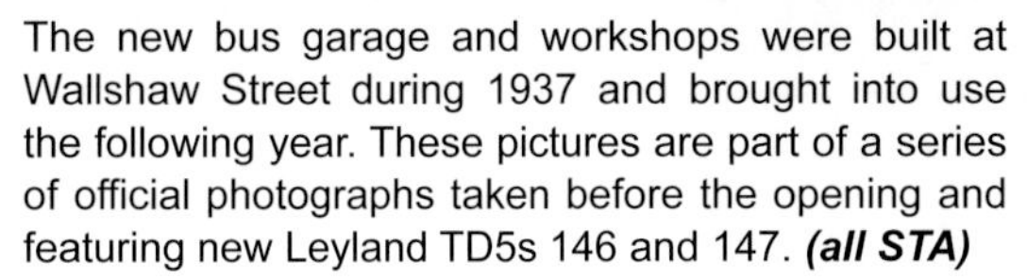

The new bus garage and workshops were built at Wallshaw Street during 1937 and brought into use the following year. These pictures are part of a series of official photographs taken before the opening and featuring new Leyland TD5s 146 and 147. ***(all STA)***

During the post-war years as new vehicles came in large numbers, many elderly buses went on to work for other owners, three of these being shown here.

William Alexander of Falkirk bought a large number of second hand buses, one such being 1935 Roe-bodied Leyland TD3 number 95 (BU 8445) in 1949. It later passed to Simpson of Roseharty in Aberdeenshire with whom it is operating in the upper picture. ***(MMT)***

Some led a harder life. 1936 Leyland TD4 number 44 (BU 9268) was withdrawn in 1950 and is pictured on the left as a circus wagon in 1952. ***(MMT)***

In the bottom picture English Electric-bodied Leyland TD5 number 150 (ABU 368), which had been withdrawn in 1954 and sold to Atkin of Ashby near Scunthorpe, stands in that town's bus station while working a local service. ***(JJH)***

Number 180 (CBU 180) was the first of the 1939 delivery of 47 Roe-bodied Leyland TD5s originally intended to replace the last of the trams. It is pictured above some ten years later at a crowded Wren's Nest on a rush hour short working on service 59. Also in the photograph are one of Manchester's new Metro-Cammell-bodied Leyland PD1/3s on the service journey and three more Oldham TD5s. ***(MMT)***

Below, one of Oldham's PD1/3s, 1947 Roe-bodied number 260 (DBU 260), rolls down Henshaw Street into the Market Place on service 11 bound for Derker. The location is unrecognisable today; all the buildings have been replaced and this part of Henshaw Street is pedestrianised. ***(STA)***

With only one low bridge in its operating area Oldham had little need for single-deckers. In the immediate post-war years these were all Crossleys which seemed a strange choice as the rest of the fleet was mostly Leyland.

In the upper picture three examples are shown parked side by side on Mainway East, Middleton to publicise the extension of service C to that point. From the left these are 1948 Roe-bodied numbers 301 (DBU 301) and 297 (DBU 297) and Crossley-bodied 364 (FBU 823) with the chrome radiator dating from 1950. ***(JJH)***

Although service E to Mossley had no low bridges on the route both Oldham and SHMD used single-deckers. Number 297 is seen again dropping down the hill into Mossley on a quiet Sunday afternoon in the 1960s. ***(AM)***

Oldham is a town built on a hill. The picture above is typical of the roads leading to the town and shows Roe-bodied Leyland PD1/3 number 272 (DBU 272) climbing up the steepest part of Chapel Road on its way to the town centre. ***(JJH)***

However, what goes up comes down and this could often be as much of a trial as climbing. In the middle picture Northern Counties-bodied Leyland PD2/30 number 441 (PBU 941), in pommard livery but displaying its SELNEC number 5341 without the logo, inches round the steep hairpin at Greenfield Station on service 10. ***(JJH)***

Water always flows to the lowest level especially after a summer cloudburst. In the lower picture the River Irk has burst its banks at Street Bridge at the bottom of the hill from Royton. The conductor of number 438 just keeps his feet dry as the driver navigates his way to the other side. This was not an unusual hazard on service 12. ***(MMT)***

North Western Road Car had a small but very important part to play in the Oldham area from as early as 1924 when the Company started running local services in Saddleworth and Crompton and into the town centre. Fifty years later, following the reorganisation of local government, its operating area in Crompton and Saddleworth became part of the expanded Oldham borough and its services were absorbed. For many years the Oldham depot was at Crofton Street off Ashton Road and the depot yard is shown in the upper picture in June 1964, buses visible including Albion Aberdonian number 716, Bristol K5G number 436 and Harrington-bodied coach number 777. ***(AM)***

Much of North Western's operating area on the eastern fringes of Oldham was open moorland with a collection of small towns and villages. Bristol L5G number 306 (DDB 298) is pictured in March 1962 passing through Delph on the infrequent service 156 from Friezland to Newhey. ***(AM)***

Upper. On the same day Willowbrook-bodied Bristol K5G number 431 (AJA 151) travels along Delph New Road on its way from Oldham to Uppermill while working the 153 circular route. This service was operated jointly with Oldham, each operator having one bus on the service. ***(AM)***

Lower. For a number of years the Bristol K5G rebodied by Willowbrook was the mainstay of North Western's services from its Oldham depot. In December 1959 the driver and conductor of number 407 (JA 7723) chat for a few minutes before leaving Greaves Street to work a journey round the Uppermill circular. ***(AM)***

Upper. At 1,100ft above sea level Grains Bar is the highest point in Oldham. In the mid-sixties when the photograph was taken it was also the county boundary and Roe-bodied Leyland PD2/30, captured on a test run, is actually in Yorkshire. The view is typical of the moorland scenery to the north and east of the town. ***(JJH)***

Lower. Still in Yorkshire but in the more sylvan scenery of the Tame Valley, new Roe-bodied Leyland PD3 number 104 (104 HBU) turns right towards Oldham at the Farrar's Arms at Grasscroft while working a service 14 journey from Uppermill to Manchester in the summer of 1964. Two Ford cars, an Anglia and a Zephyr, approach the junction from the opposite direction. ***(STA)***

Upper. Between Shaw and Newhey, Jubilee Bridge crosses what was once the Oldham to Rochdale railway line, soon to become part of the Manchester Metrolink network. A notorious accident spot, Atlantean number 145 (GBU 145D) negotiates it on its way to Manchester. ***(JJH)***

Lower. The lift bridge over the Rochdale Canal at Middleton Junction was known locally as 'The Donger' from the noise made by vehicles crossing the iron plates of the decking. Marshall-bodied Leyland Tiger Cub number 111 (111 JBU) crosses the bridge on a service C journey from Middleton Junction to Higginshaw in 1966. In the background can just be seen a Leyland PD2 standing at the terminus of service B at Middleton Junction station. ***(JJH)***

Above. A typical scene on Yorkshire Street in the mid-sixties. East Lancashire-bodied Leyland Atlantean number 133 (GBU 133D) climbs the hill towards the Market Place on a service 98 journey while behind an elderly Manchester Leyland PD2/6 follows it on service 82. A Bedford van passes in the opposite direction while an Austin car is parked at the front of a line of vehicles where now there are double yellow lines. Yorkshire Street is now one-way in the direction away from the camera.***(STA)***

Left. Roe-bodied version number 167 (OBU 167F) stands on Piccadilly Station Approach, Manchester, ready to work a trip on the long 59 service to Shaw. The station has since been modernised and the area is now restricted to minibuses on the Manchester Metroshuttle services. ***(STA)***

Above. Public transport is all about people. In this evocative picture taken in March 1950, most of the population of the Strinesdale Estate plus the local brass band turn out in the early morning sunshine to welcome the arrival of the bus service for which they have been waiting three years. ***(MMT)***

Right. Buses don't drive themselves. The crew of Leyland Tiger Cub number 116 (116 JBU) stand proudly in front of their new bus at Shore Edge before leaving on the short, semi-rural journey to Royton. ***(JJH)***

Above. The making of a star. Tiger Cub number 113 (113 JBU) is filmed by a television crew on the moors above Denshaw. ***(STA)***

Upper left. Since 1961 Oldham has been twinned with the town of Kranj in Slovenia, the corporation providing transport. Here number 111 (111 JBU) is being suitably labelled in the paint shop. The rebodied number 299 stands in the background. ***(STA)***

Lower left. An essential member of the fleet is the tow wagon, seen here towing Leyland PD1 number 232 into the workshops. ***(JJH)***

Opposite page upper. New Atlantean number 146 (GBU 146D) on the Roe stand at the 1966 Commercial Motor Show. ***(MMT)***

Opposite page lower. In 1925 the LMS Railway imposed a 5-ton weight limit on the bridge over the Lees line on Park Road. Oldham ignored it and in the late forties British Railways replaced the board with a brand new one. The railway line and the bridge are long gone and buses still run along Park Road today. ***(MMT)***

OLDHAM
PRV 1967
Private

BRITISH RAILWAYS
NOTICE IS HEREBY GIVEN THAT THIS
BRIDGE IS INSUFFICENT TO CARRY,
A VEHICLE THE WEIGHT LOADED
EXCEEDS 5 TONS
AND THAT VEHICLES IN EXCESS OF SUCH
WEIGHT MUST NOT CROSS THE BRIDGE
ANY PERSON CAUSING DAMAGE
BY NON-COMPLIANCE WITH THIS
NOTICE WILL BE HELD LIABLE THEREFOR.
BY ORDER

Upper. Several examples of Oldham buses are preserved. Perhaps best known is number 246 (DBU 246), a Roe-bodied Leyland PD1/3 dating from 1947. It was the oldest Oldham bus to pass to SELNEC and is now preserved at the Greater Manchester Museum of Transport at Boyle Street, Cheetham. ***(JAS)***

Lower. Crossley double-decker number 368 (FBU 827) was bought by the omnibus branch of the Buckley Wells Railway Enthusiasts' Association in 1968 for £40. It later passed to the Crossley Omnibus Society at Tameside and is now resident at Boyle Street. ***(STA)***

Above. Roe-bodied Leyland PD2/30 number 394 (NBU 494) dates from 1957. It became a driver trainer and when withdrawn in 1978 was the last Oldham bus to carry the Pommard livery. It is pictured in the depot next to Greater Manchester Metrobus number 5006. ***(STA)***

Upper right. Atlantean number 163 (OBU 163F), new in 1968, was withdrawn in 1981 and was purchased by a local morris troupe. It is now owned by the Bury Bus Group and is seen here at the Peak Park Preserved Bus Gathering in June 2011. ***(JAS)***

Lower right. One that didn't make it. Leyland PD1 number 231 (DBU 23) was bought for preservation in 1967 but became derelict and was eventually broken up. It is seen in Wallshaw Street parked next to the author's minivan DBU 23C. ***(CR)***

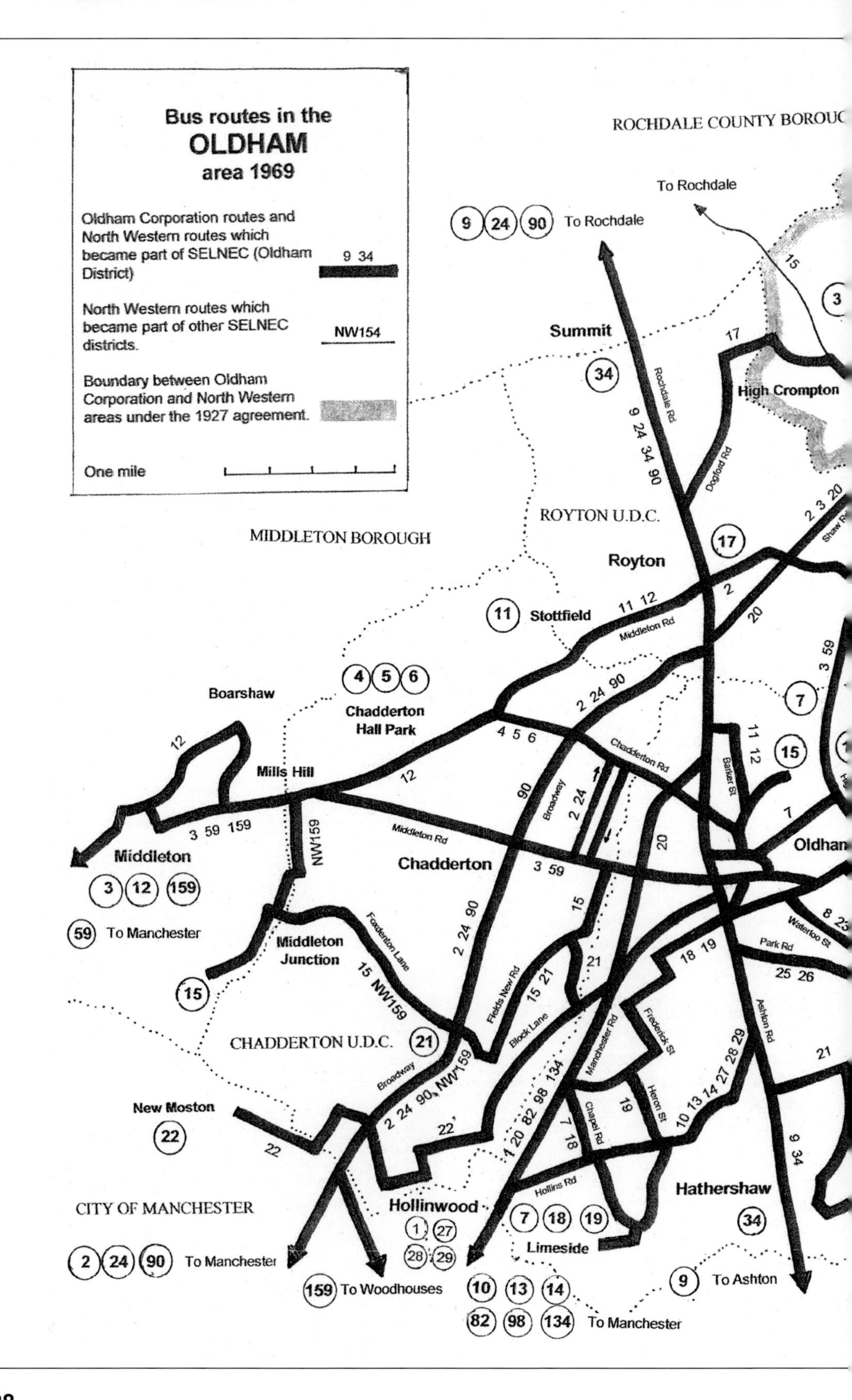
Bus routes in the
OLDHAM
area 1969
Oldham Corporation routes and North Western routes which became part of SELNEC (Oldham District)
9 34
North Western routes which became part of other SELNEC districts.
NW154
Boundary between Oldham Corporation and North Western areas under the 1927 agreement.
One mile
ROCHDALE COUNTY BOROUGH
To Rochdale
9 24 90 To Rochdale
Summit
34
High Crompton
ROYTON U.D.C.
MIDDLETON BOROUGH
Royton
Stottfield
Chadderton Hall Park
Boarshaw
Mills Hill
Middleton
3 12 159
59 To Manchester
Middleton Junction
Chadderton
Oldham
CHADDERTON U.D.C.
New Moston
CITY OF MANCHESTER
Hollinwood
Limeside
Hathershaw
2 24 90 To Manchester
159 To Woodhouses
10 13 14 82 98 134 To Manchester
9 To Ashton
Rochdale Rd
Dogford Rd
Middleton Rd
Chadderton Rd
Broadway
Barker St
Foxdenton Lane
Fields New Rd
Block Lane
Manchester Rd
Frederick St
Heron St
Chapel Rd
Hollins Rd
Ashton Rd
Waterloo St
Park Rd
Shaw Rd

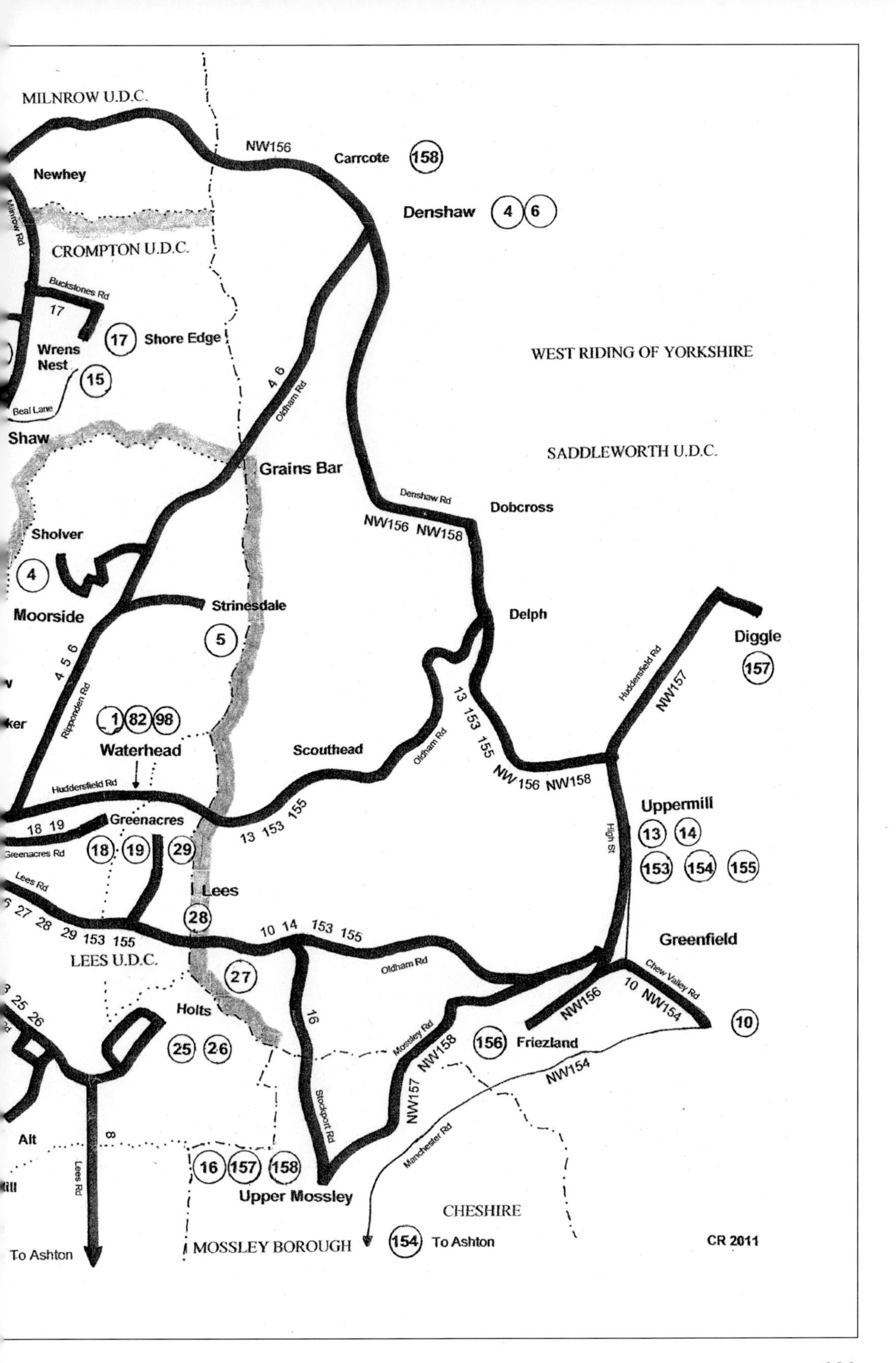
MILNROW U.D.C.
NW156
Carrcote
158
Newhey
Denshaw
4
6
Milnrow Rd
CROMPTON U.D.C.
Buckstones Rd
17
17
Shore Edge
Wrens Nest
15
Beal Lane
WEST RIDING OF YORKSHIRE
4 6
Oldham Rd
Shaw
SADDLEWORTH U.D.C.
Grains Bar
Denshaw Rd
Dobcross
NW156 NW158
Sholver
4
Moorside
Strinesdale
Delph
5
Diggle
157
4 5 6
Huddersfield Rd
NW157
Ripponden Rd
13 153 155
1 82 98
Oldham Rd
Waterhead
Scouthead
NW156 NW158
Huddersfield Rd
Uppermill
18 19
Greenacres
13 153 155
High St
13
14
Greenacres Rd
18
19
29
153
154
155
Lees Rd
Lees
28
27 28 29 153 155
10 14 153 155
Greenfield
LEES U.D.C.
Oldham Rd
Chew Valley Rd
27
NW156
10 NW154
25 26
Holts
16
10
25
26
Mossley Rd
156
Friezland
NW158
NW157
NW154
Stockport Rd
Manchester Rd
Alt
8
Lees Rd
16
157
158
Upper Mossley
CHESHIRE
To Ashton
MOSSLEY BOROUGH
154
To Ashton
CR 2011

Although 90 years separate these two pictures of Rhodes Bank there have only been superficial changes during that time. In the scene above, in the spring of 1921, passengers enjoy a ride on the open balcony as a tram drifts down Yorkshire Street. ***(STA)*** In the lower picture taken in September 2011 the buildings have had a facelift but are otherwise largely unchanged. The underground toilets have gone and the yellow board tells us that Oldham is open as usual during Metrolink construction. Yorkshire Street is now one way towards the camera and traffic in the other direction goes along Union Street, and the tram has been replaced by a medley of First Manchester Volvos. ***(CR)***

If the preceding pair of photographs shows little change then these two taken from the same spot in West Street could not be more different. Some time in the late fifties Crossley single-decker number 292 (DBU 292) is shown in the upper picture working a service C journey to Middleton Junction, the area across the road cleared for redevelopment. ***(MMT)*** Below, in August 2011, none of the old buildings remain and the Civic Centre rises on the left. The Corporation buses are no more and a First Manchester Volvo passes the new bus station buildings on its way to Bury via Middleton on service 58. ***(CR)***

In the upper picture taken in the early sixties, Crossley double-decker number 367 (FBU 826) passes the General Post Office on Union Street while in the background a Roe-bodied Leyland PD1 turns right into Waterloo Street. ***(STA)*** Some fifty years later Union Street is little changed although the Post Office building now houses the Local Studies Library and Archives while the bus pulling away from the stop is a First Manchester Volvo on the long service 59 to Manchester. ***(CR)***

Momentous changes are taking place at Mumps in this pair of pictures. In the middle sixties new Roe-bodied Leyland PD3 number 103 (103 HBU) turns out of Lees Road and passes under the railway bridge on its way in from Grotton. ***(AM)*** By October 2011 the bridge has gone and the area is being cleared for the new Metrolink line. Another of First Manchester's large fleet of Volvo double-deckers rounds the corner into Mumps on service 184 from Uppermill to Manchester. ***(CR)***

Oldham only bought one batch of Daimlers after the war. These were 25 CVD6s, ten bodied by Roe and 15 by Crossley delivered between 1948 and 1949. One of the Crossley-bodied buses, a tired-looking number 330 (EBU 930), stands (above) in the depot yard in 1965. It would be withdrawn from service and broken up a few months later. ***(JJH)***

A mud-spattered number 362 (FBU 821), one of a batch of four all-Crossley SD42/7 single-deckers new in 1950 is pictured (below) at the same location shortly before withdrawal in 1965. ***(JJH)***

Thirty-one Leyland PD2/20s were delivered during 1957 carrying a mix of Roe, Crossley and Northern Counties bodies. Two of the Roe versions are shown here. In the upper picture number 389 (NBU 489) waits at the Rushcroft terminus of service 3 when new while below number 391 (NBU 491) stands in Car Street, between the workshops and the depot, after its withdrawal from service in 1973 and subsequent transfer to driver training duty as SELNEC's TV3. ***(both JJH)***

In 1963 Roe-bodied Leyland PD2/20 number 402 (NBU 502) was painted in experimental two-tone blue inspired by a Manchester airport-liveried Tiger Cub which had been borrowed a few months earlier. Number 402 is pictured above in the original version with a yellow band beneath the lower deck windows and below outside Alexandra Park with the yellow band removed and a white band substituted between decks. ***(both JJH)***

Above. Number 424 (PBU 924) was a Metro-Cammell-bodied Leyland PD2/30 dating from 1958. Pictured in the depot in early PTE days it displays its already grimy orange. It would be withdrawn in 1974. ***(JJH)***

Right upper. Standing in Manchester's Stevenson Square on service 24 early in 1970 is number 450 (PBU 950), another Leyland PD2/30 this time with Northern Counties body. It carries its new number 5350 but no insignia and would not have received the orange livery being withdrawn the following year. ***(JJH)***

Right lower. Number 463 (LWE 104) was a 1949 Leyland PD2/1 bought from the Sheffield Joint Omnibus Committee in 1965 as a temporary expedient. It survived into SELNEC days and was allocated the number 5363 although it never carried it, being withdrawn in 1969. ***(MMT)***

Two views of the elegant but largely unloved Roe-bodied Leyland PD3/5s introduced in 1964. In the upper picture number 101 (101 HBU), the first of the batch of ten, stands at the Newhey terminus of service 2. This windswept open space also served as the terminus for Rochdale's services but it would be many years before a re-casting of the network in PTE days introduced through running across Newhey. Soon to be withdrawn, number 5104 (104 HBU) is pictured below at Mumps looking decidedly down at heel in its faded orange SELNEC livery. ***(both JJH)***

Six Leyland Tiger Cubs were purchased in 1964/65 to replace the ageing Crossley single-deckers and enable their routes to be converted to driver-only operation. The first four were bodied by Marshall and the remaining two by the local firm of Pennine Coachcraft. Number 111 (111 JBU), the first of the batch with a Marshall body, is seen in the upper photograph passing under Mumps Bridge. ***(MMT)***

Six Marshall-bodied Leyland Panthers were delivered in 1968 to convert more routes. Number 175 (OBU 175F) is shown below when new. ***(MMT)***

After the ten PD3s no more front-engined buses were bought new and further double-deck orders were for Atlanteans mostly with Roe bodies. Number 129 (CBU 129C), poses for its official photograph when new. The ten buses of this batch were the last to be delivered in the traditional crimson lake and white livery. ***(JJH)***

Number 146 (GBU 146D), a Neepsend-bodied variant, enters the gloomy recesses of Wallshaw Place on its way to Holts Estate, followed by another unidentified Atlantean on service T to Grotton. ***(JJH)***

Above. Atlantean Number 171 (OBU 171F) was the first Oldham bus to wear the new SELNEC colours when at the end of 1969 one bus from each of the former operators was painted and shown off to the media on the Hyde Road training school yard. ***(MMT)***

Upper right. Five Roe-bodied Atlanteans were delivered early in 1970 carrying SELNEC fleet numbers but in Oldham livery. Number 5186 (WBU 186H) is shown turning from Wildmoor Avenue into Lees New Road on its way from Holts Estate to Oldham. ***(JJH)***

Lower right. In 1981 the PTE revised its livery with more orange and a brown skirt. Number 5188 (ABU 188J), was mistakenly painted in the new colour scheme although due to be withdrawn in a few weeks. It therefore became the only former Oldham bus to carry the new livery and is seen here in the depot in all its splendour but with fleet numbers and logo blacked out and carrying the registration plates from withdrawn No. 5180 to hide its identity. ***(JJH)***

Atlantean number 163 (OBU 163F) was withdrawn and initially passed to the Darronettes Morris Troupe of Oldham but was later rescued for preservation by the Bury Bus Group. ***(JAS)***

The immaculate 246 (DBU 246), a Roe-bodied Leyland PD1/3 dating from 1947, was the oldest Oldham Corporation bus taken into the SELNEC fleet in 1969. It was allocated number 5246 but never carried it and was withdrawn in 1970. It is now preserved at the Greater Manchester Museum of Transport at Boyle Street, Cheetham. ***(both JJH)***

Above. Number 460 (PBU 960), a Leyland PD2/30 with Northern Counties body, was delivered to Oldham in January 1959. It became SELNEC 5360 and was withdrawn in 1971 and sold to Paton of Renfrew, in whose colours it is pictured. ***(JJH)***

Upper left. Atlantean GBU 141D was originally Oldham number 141 delivered in 1966. It was withdrawn as Greater Manchester Transport 5141 in 1979 and passed to Ede of Par in Cornwall, later moving across the country to Bowman of Birtley in Tyne and Wear where it is pictured. ***(JJH)***

Lower left. Atlantean number 149 (LBU 149E) dated from 1967. It became SELNEC 5149 and was withdrawn in 1980 when it was donated to the Manchester Youth Community Service. In this latter guise it is seen parked at the back of Northenden Garage. ***(MMT)***